Faith Traditions and the Family

Faith Traditions and the Family

Phyllis D. Airhart
Margaret Lamberts Bendroth
editors

Westminster John Knox Press
Louisville, Kentucky

Scripture quotations, unless otherwise indicated, are from the New Revised Standard Version of the Bible, copyright © 1989 by the Division of Christian Education of the National Council of the Churches of Christ in the U.S.A., and used by permission.

Book and cover design by Jennifer K. Cox

First edition

Published by Westminster John Knox Press
Louisville, Kentucky

This book is printed on acid-free paper that meets the American National Standards Institute Z39.48 standard. ⊚

PRINTED IN THE UNITED STATES OF AMERICA

96 97 98 99 00 01 02 03 04 05 — 10 9 8 7 6 5 4 3 2 1

Library of Congress Cataloging-in-Publication Data

Faith traditions and the family / edited by Phyllis D. Airhart and
    Margaret Lamberts Bendroth — 1st ed.
        p.   cm. — (The family, religion, and culture)
    Includes bibliographical references.
    ISBN 0-664-25581-7 (alk. paper)
    1. Family—Religious life. 2. Church work with families.
3. Family—North America.   I. Airhart, Phyllis D., date.
II. Bendroth, Margaret Lamberts, date.   III. Series.
BV4526.2.F314   1996
261.8'3585—dc20   96-16562

Contents

Series Foreword

There is an important debate going on today over the present health and future well-being of families in American society. Although some people on the political right and left use this debate primarily to further partisan causes, the debate is real, and it is over genuine issues. The debate, however, is not well informed and is riddled with historical, theological, and social-scientific ignorance.

This is not unusual as political debates go. The American family debate, however, is especially uninformed and dogmatic. This is understandable, for all people have experienced a family in some way, feel themselves to be experts, and believe that they are entitled to their strong opinions.

The books in this series, The Family, Religion, and Culture, discuss these issues in ways that will place the American debate about the family on more solid ground. The series is the result of the Religion, Culture, and Family Project, which was funded by a generous grant from the Division of Religion of the Lilly Endowment, Inc. and was located at the Institute for Advanced Study in The University of Chicago Divinity School. Part of the project proceeded while Don Browning, the project director, was in residence at the Center of Theological Inquiry at Princeton, New Jersey.

The series advances no single point of view on this debate and gives no one solution. The authors and editors contributing to the volumes represent both genders as well as a variety of religious and ethnic perspectives and denominational backgrounds—liberal and conservative; Protestant, Catholic, and Jewish; evangelical and mainline; and black, white, and Asian. Several of the authors and editors met annually for a seminar and discussed—often with considerable intensity—their outlines, papers, and chapters pertaining to the various books. The careful reader will notice that many of the seminar members did influence one another; but, it is safe to say, each of them in the end took their own counsel and spoke out of their own convictions.

The series is comprehensive, with studies on the family in ancient Is-
rael and early Christianity; on economics and the family, law, feminism,
and reproductive technology and the family; the family and American
faith traditions; congregations and families; and two summary books—
one a handbook; the other, a critical overview of the American family
debate.

This book, *Faith Traditions and the Family,* tells the stories of several
North American religious traditions and their struggle over the last
decades to respond to the emerging debate over the family. After reading the book, one commentator said, "I felt as though I were on top of
a mountain with the American religious landscape on matters of sex and
family spread before me below." The reader will gain a commanding
overview of the differing roads that North American traditions have
traveled regarding these issues.

All of these denominations and traditions have faced the disruptive
forces of modernization—the rise of technical reason, the spread of
market forces, the increased involvement of government in our lives,
and the rising educational levels of church members. In spite of being
faced with very similar social forces, these traditions *made different decisions.* The forces of modernization as such did not dictate the responses of these denominations.

Readers will leave these chapters with their vision expanded, will find
that no one tradition has a corner on the truth, and finally will conclude
that North American traditions can learn much from one another. Both
the conservative and liberal, the evangelical and mainline, black and
white, and the Protestant and Catholic should now come to know what
each of them are doing in facing the family crisis. No one will read this
book without finding new ideas relevant to a fresh rethinking of the
family practices of their own religious tradition.

Don S. Browning
Ian S. Evison

Acknowledgments

By the time a book like this one nears completion, it is, in every sense, a group effort. Don Browning, Ian Evison, and John Wall of the Religion, Culture, and Family Project first conceived the design for this book, advocated for its necessity, and cheered its completion. Other friends and colleagues helped us locate the wonderful authors whose work we are so pleased to present in the following pages: many thanks to Scott Appleby, Myron Augsburger, Paula Datsko Barker, Ross Bender, Edith Blumhofer, Lisa Sowle Cahill, Janet Forsyth Fishburn, Robert Franklin, Robert Handy, Susannah Heschel, Bryan Hillis, Martin Marty, Jan Shipps, and Mary Stewart Van Leeuwen.

We are also thankful to the staff of the Bursar's Office at Victoria University, University of Toronto, for handling innumerable financial details with careful efficiency. Emmanuel College's Centre for the Study of Religion in Canada facilitated a pleasant and productive meeting of contributors in April 1994. Heather Gamester, our indefatigable copyeditor, deserves much gratitude for bringing eleven disparate chapters into the shape of a single volume. At Westminster John Knox Press, Timothy Staveteig, Stephanie Egnotovich, and Lorene K. Johnson guided our manuscript through a sea of last minute details with patience and humor.

And although it seems a bit obvious for a book like this one to be dedicated to the authors' families, we don't think that it will hurt to say it one more time. Nathan Bendroth, who waited for his mother to come home from the Toronto meeting before having a life-threatening allergic reaction, reminds us all of the infinite preciousness and terrifying fragility of family ties. We all write within the ongoing lives of our families, and we remember each one with gratitude.

Contributors

PHYLLIS D. AIRHART is Associate Professor of History of Christianity at Emmanuel College of Victoria University (University of Toronto) in Ontario, Canada. She is author of *Serving the Present Age: Revivalism, Progressivism, and the Methodist Tradition in Canada* as well as articles on religion and culture in Canada.

DAPHNE J. ANDERSON has served both as volunteer and staff person to the Native Ministries Program at Vancouver School of Theology in British Columbia, Canada. She is an active layperson both ecumenically and within the United Church of Canada.

TERENCE R. ANDERSON is Professor of Christian Ethics at Vancouver School of Theology in British Columbia, Canada. A consultant on social issues, including healthcare ethics and advocacy for First Nations peoples, he is the author of *Walking the Way: Christian Ethics as a Guide*.

MARGARET LAMBERTS BENDROTH is Co-Director of Women and Twentieth Century Protestantism Project at Andover Newton Theological Seminary, Newton Centre, Massachusetts. She is author of *Fundamentalism and Gender, 1875 to the Present* and numerous articles on women and conservative Protestantism.

CLAUDIA L. BUSHMAN teaches American Studies at Columbia University in New York. She is currently working on a study of John Walker, an antebellum Virginia farmer. She is author of *America Discovers Columbus: How an Italian Explorer Became an American Hero* and *"A Good Poor Man's Wife": Being the Chronicle of Harriet Hanson Robinson and Her Family in Nineteenth-Century New England* as well as editor of *Mormon Sisters: Women in Early Utah*.

RICHARD L. BUSHMAN is Gouverneur Morris Professor of History at Columbia University in New York. His writings include *From Puritan to Yankee: Character and the Social Order in Connecticut, 1670–1765; Joseph Smith and the Beginnings of Mormonism; King and People in Provincial Massachusetts;* and *The Refinement of America: Persons, Houses, Cities.*

WILLIAM P. DEVEAUX is pastor of Metropolitan African Methodist Episcopal Church in Washington, D.C., and has taught at Vanderbilt University, The Divinity School in Nashville, Tennessee, Howard University School of Divinity in Washington, D.C., and Wesley Theological Seminary in Washington, D.C. His writings include articles on Richard Allen's social policy and the social thought of Martin Luther King, Jr.

SYLVIA BARACK FISHMAN is Assistant Professor of Contemporary American Jewish Life in the Near Eastern and Judaic Studies Department at Brandeis University in Waltham, Massachusetts. She is author of *A Breath of Life: Feminism in the American Jewish Community; Follow My Footsteps: Changing Images of Women in American Jewish Fiction;* and *Changing Lifestyles of American Jewish Women and Men* (forthcoming).

WILLIAM R. GARRETT is Professor of Sociology at St. Michael's College in Colchester, Vermont. He is the author of *Seasons of Marriage and Family Life;* editor of *Social Consequences of Religious Belief;* and co-editor with Roland Robertson of *Religion and Global Order.* His numerous articles on the sociology of religion include studies of familial transformation and the process of globalization.

JOANNA BOWEN GILLESPIE is co-founder of the Episcopal Women's History Project and Adjunct Professor of Church and Society at Bangor Theological Seminary in Hanover, New Hampshire. She is author of *Women Speak of God, Congregations, and Change* as well as numerous articles exploring the inter-relatedness of women, education, family, social class, and religion.

CHRISTINE FIRER HINZE is Assistant Professor of Theological Ethics at Marquette University in Milwaukee, Wisconsin. She is author of *Comprehending Power in Christian Social Ethics* as well as articles on Catholic economic thought and feminist Christian ethics.

J. HOWARD KAUFFMAN is Professor Emeritus of Sociology at Goshen College in Goshen, Indiana. He is the co-author with Leland Harder of *Anabaptists Four Centuries Later: A Profile of Five Mennonite and Brethren in Christ Denominations* and with Leo Driedger of *The Mennonite Mosaic: Identity and Modernization.*

BILL J. LEONARD is Dean of the Divinity School at Wake Forest University, Winston-Salem, North Carolina. He is the author of *The Word of God Across the Ages; God's Last and Only Hope: The Fragmentation of the*

Southern Baptist Convention; and *Risk the Journey: Answering God's Call to Proclaim His Word.* He is also the editor of *Becoming Christian: Dimensions of Spiritual Formation* and *Dictionary of Baptists in America.*

EILEEN W. LINDNER is Associate General Secretary for Christian Unity, National Council of Churches of Christ in the U.S.A. A church historian who has written on the social gospel movement, she is the primary author of *When Churches Mind the Children* as well as numerous articles on child advocacy.

GAIL E. MURPHY-GEISS is an ordained United Methodist minister and a Ph.D. candidate in Religion and Social Change at the Iliff School of Theology in Denver, Colorado.

JEAN MILLER SCHMIDT is Professor of Modern Church History at Iliff School of Theology in Denver, Colorado. She is author of *Souls or the Social Order: The Two-Party System in American Protestantism,* co-editor of *Perspectives on American Methodism: Interpretive Essays,* and author of the forthcoming book *Grace Sufficient: A History of Women in American Methodism.*

Introduction:
Churches and Families
in North American Society

PHYLLIS D. AIRHART
MARGARET LAMBERTS BENDROTH

F ew issues have the power to generate controversy like the future of the contemporary family. Add religion, and the mix becomes even more complex and, oftener than not, combustible. While some religious bodies ardently defend the "traditional family," others have just as strongly denounced its potential for harboring abusive relationships. Indeed, in recent decades religious leaders have expressed an abundance of concern, but have offered no single answer to the growing debate over the past meaning, present purpose, and future prospects of the family in North American society.

When Don Browning invited us to join the Religion, Culture, and Family project, he offered the daunting task of exploring the role of North American denominations in this complex controversy. We responded by inviting knowledgeable persons from a number of different religious bodies to describe and analyze the way their respective traditions have thought about families over the last half century. We asked them to relate what their different traditions have both said and done about family issues, to delineate important shifts in policy, and to suggest some of the consequences. We wanted to know how family-related policies and programs played out in different denominational stories of growth and decline, and we asked our authors to reflect on the relative roles of theology, scriptural authority, and the social sciences in the theory and practice of family life. We asked them to describe the range of voices within their own traditions—progressive, conservative, and anything in between—and to assess their relative impact on family-related issues.

The result is a diverse collection of chapters that address a similar set of questions from a variety of distinct perspectives. Our contributors represent a range of religious traditions, from conservative to liberal.

Not only do they present insiders' views of the diversity within their own ranks, but also offer the eclectic perspectives of historians, sociologists, ethicists, ministers, and lay members of local congregations. They also have drawn on wide-ranging sources for their analysis, including church policy statements, survey data, and denominational magazines.

Predictably ours is not an exhaustive catalog of denominational responses to family issues, nor even a representative survey of different positions. Although the chapters record the well-publicized debates in mainstream churches about marriage, sexuality, and the future of the nuclear family, they also reveal lesser-known but equally important aspects of the discussion as it is being carried on in other circles.

The aim of our selection is to illuminate significant aspects of the larger conversation. We have included, for example, the largely urban Jewish faith along with the more markedly rural Mennonites. Regional and national dynamics shape the narratives of the Southern Baptists and the United Church of Canada. Ethnicity and class are important themes for groups as socially diverse as Episcopalians, African Methodists, and Roman Catholics. Other groups, Mormons in particular, exemplify a highly conscious family-centered theology and practice. Our narrative also includes a comparison of two important church agencies, the National Council of the Churches of Christ in the United States and the National Association of Evangelicals, highlighting the theological rationales behind different attitudes toward government involvement in family issues.

The first and most decisive impression is that the neat and static picture of public versus private, liberal versus conservative that many associate with a "culture wars" typology is not adequate. We found instead a broad range of institutional responses to a strikingly similar set of challenges. As these chapters show so clearly, no single group can claim "ownership" of family issues; much soul-searching and hard work has been done by all.

Some distinct themes emerge. All of the accounts, for example, revolve around similar changes in the relationship between church and family over the past fifty years. The transformation has involved broad issues of individualism and community, normative definitions of family, shifting definitions in sexual ethics, and the changing role of denominational structures described in the following section. In the final section of this introduction we will push this descriptive analysis toward some broader concluding themes and attempt to chart some general insights about the future direction of the debate on family.

The Changing
North American Family

One message common to all the chapters is the undisputed impact of modernity. The growing individualism and fragmentation of family life stand in sharp contrast with the ideal of community, something that all groups applaud but picture in different ways. Some believe community should support the inviolable privacy of the individual conscience; others uplift the integrity and moral sanctity of the community over against the individual. For example, some groups envision community as a voluntary "support group," viewing such family-related issues as divorce, abortion, and the religious formation of children as essentially private matters. In the mainstream Protestant churches, which often typify this position, toleration is the watchword, and the frequent result a loss of consensus and an inability to speak with one voice. Other theological traditions uphold the givenness of community, a *Gemeinschaft* that sets and upholds norms that shape behavior. Groups as theologically diverse as Mennonites and Mormons often protect their boundaries by maintaining more-than-subtle pressure on their members.

The cultural plurality associated with modernity is not alone in fostering tensions between individualism and community. The materialism generated by capitalism's market economy has also had a corrosive effect on family life. Christopher Lasch, for example, argues that the invasion of the market into family life has had a devastating effect on families. The desires of a consumer-oriented society "wore away at the moral foundations of family life" by making money the primary measure of value.[1] Such economic considerations are often overlooked by those who would connect a family "crisis" with women seeking personal liberation and growth through work outside the home—an example of how economic forces complicate definitions of the "successful" family.

The seductiveness of self-interest and rational choice in economic considerations presents a dilemma for family advocates. Is it possible to present the family as integral to a fulfilling life and also acknowledge its very real problems? Studies on family breakdowns present parents and their children as a group, concluding that children from intact families fare better than those raised by single parents or in homes broken by divorce. But what of the individual cases that so often make up denominational policy—husbands and wives in soul-destroying or abusive marriages, and others in good marriages facing hard decisions about professional careers and childrearing?

The challenge for religious leaders is to find within their tradition ways to present positive but realistic images of parenting and family life, to make them integral to the "good life" and to offer practical resources to make its attainment possible. A number of the chapters in this volume suggest that the formation, subsistence, and stability of the family have become peripheral to personal fulfillment, making it easier to rationalize leaving an unhappy marriage or to make excuses for skirting parental obligations. The recent focus on *fathering* in some denominations is in part an attempt to reconnect self-actualization with responsibility. It remains to be seen whether the "pro-male" stance of such groups as Promise Keepers can press for the ·importance of fathering without becoming at the same time antifeminist.

The chapters in this volume suggest that one of the most significant developments of recent decades is the growing separation of sexuality and marriage from procreation and family. This is not just a trend in secular society. It is happening in many religious traditions and their policies reflect their attempts to cope with and to accommodate these developments. These issues are presented most provocatively in the chapter on the United Church of Canada, but this trend pervades analysis of other denominations as well. Not only in real life, but in many denominational policy statements, intimacy, self-fulfillment and self-actualization have become primary; children are now, to quote that famous line from Murphy Brown, "just another lifestyle choice" that involves obligation only once selected. The language of those documents suggests that "family" is no longer taken for granted, nor does it invariably assume different obligations for men and women—obligations no longer regarded as acceptable for couples who seek a mutuality not always presupposed by the older model.

For now, denominations remain the most visible organizational expression of religious life in North America. But what of the future? Are parishes, congregations, or "special purpose" organizations supplanting them?[2] If so, do denominations still have a role to play in articulating a moral vision that will make a difference in discussions of the future of the family?

Declining denominational influence in family-related issues is a particularly striking note throughout this book. Evangelicals, for example, are as likely to turn for advice on family issues to Focus on the Family as to their denomination. In matters of public policy—abortion, for example—special purpose groups play at least as prominent a role as do official church policies. This is one more example of the impact of modernity and a market-driven culture: culture-affirming and culture-denying groups alike display a constituency-driven consumer response to family issues.

Taken in sum, these chapters call for repairing the rift between important aspects of family life too easily separated: private and public, individual and community, personal fulfillment and family responsibility. No one group holds the solution to *re-pairing* the family; however, in the collective wisdom of our traditions we have much to learn from each other. The chapters in this volume certainly do not present any simple formula for success in the family arena. The picture they have drawn is far too complex to support normative prescriptions or one-dimensional analyses. They do, however, point toward some general conclusions about the past, present, and future in the ongoing debate on religion and the family.

Effective Church Strategies: Some Concluding Observations

The most powerful insight these chapters offer is the necessity of negotiating with, rather than rejecting, modernity. None of the groups represented in this volume has managed to avoid the manifold changes affecting families in the decades following World War II, despite a certain amount of rhetoric to the contrary. But many of them did try to provide ways for their members to sort out and prioritize secular demands on family life. For example, in the matter of material success, the Mormon leaders described in chapter 2 reminded working fathers of the postwar era that "no other success can compensate for failure in the home." This well-worn phrase put hardworking young professionals on notice that their personal ambition was not wrong, but it must be tempered by responsibility.

The other example is feminism. As our chapters suggest, the complicated changes in women's economic and social status following World War II affected even the most conservative religious cultures; survival, however, did not depend on resisting or rejecting feminism. As Howard Kauffman demonstrates in chapter 3, egalitarian marriages, two-career couples, and shared housekeeping are commonplace for Mennonites yet feminism remains a controversial—and highly symbolic—issue, as is the case for other socially conservative religious bodies. However, the conflict may not be as deep-seated as it often appears to outsiders.

Indeed, denominational struggles in the family arena rarely result in unconditional victories. The ongoing task, as these chapters define it, is to celebrate, protect, educate, and sustain families whether or not the surrounding culture supports such efforts. This means upholding the home as a viable site for worship, religious training, and spiritual formation, as well as maintaining theological and institutional systems that welcome families—especially children—taking them seriously, resisting the urge to sentimentalize them, problematize them, or reduce them to ethical abstractions. The family thus remains an interpretive lens through which to evaluate the ethical issues that have made such huge demands on the time and attention of religious leaders since the 1960s. In this sense, then, an effective family strategy is not a state to be achieved, but a stance that is consistently maintained over time, sometimes at considerable cost. And the task is becoming increasingly complex.

Some denominations have managed to maintain a certain amount of cohesiveness through a distinct ethnic, racial, or regional identity. Moreover, many have kept alive the memory of costly struggle—racial prejudice, religious persecution—that has made them wary of the dominant culture. Some retain metaphors of identity and togetherness, like the ethnic parish for Roman Catholics or the westward trek for Mormons. Others value community life for explicit theological reasons.

All of the groups, however, currently face challenges that threaten to overwhelm traditional loyalties. Urban poverty as well as upward mobility have fractured once-cohesive religious communities; no group remains immune from the crisis of authority that has affected rural Southern Baptists, urban blacks, and upper-class Episcopalians alike. Still, as the chapters in this book show so well, distinct theological and cultural traditions can and do provide significant resources in the face of these challenges. Jean Miller Schmidt, for example, finds John Wesley's emphasis on "grace full and free" guiding present-day United Methodist discussions of divorce and homosexuality. William Garrett, in chapter 8, depicts an ongoing dialectic between the denomination's historic emphasis on doctrinal and ecclesial authority and the demands of modern society, contrasting the magisterial voice of church leaders of the 1920s with the increasingly accommodationist stance of recent decades.

None of our authors predict a rosy future; some even adopt a despairing tone. But together the chapters suggest that conflict may not necessarily indicate failure. For groups committed to engaging modernity on their own terms, controversy may be a sign of institutional resilience, as well as an occasion for theological creativity. If this is so, it may be a price well worth paying.

"We must always walk into the future with an eye on the past." So goes a famous legal maxim that John Witte, a coparticipant in the Religious, Culture, and Family project, is fond of quoting. To those who care about faith and the family, the contributors to this volume have provided a window through which we can view the past as we walk into the future. Too often the religious voices represented here have been heard in isolation. The stories we present in this volume suggest that there is much to be gained by continuing the conversation.

NOTES

1. Christopher Lasch, *The Revolt of the Elites and the Betrayal of Democracy* (New York: W. W. Norton, 1995), 95–96.
2. Robert Wuthnow, *The Restructuring of American Religion* (Princeton: Princeton University Press, 1988), 71–99.

1

Southern Baptist:
Family as Witness of Grace
in the Community

BILL J. LEONARD

When *Home Life,* a Christian family magazine, first appeared in 1947, the introduction described the challenges facing the post-war family and the need for such a Baptist periodical. Clifton J. Allen, executive secretary of the Sunday School Board of the Southern Baptist Convention (SBC), wrote that

> one out of five homes crashes on the rocks of divorce. Family life is being blighted by strong drink, lust, and worldly pleasure. Happiness is driven from literally millions of homes by misunderstanding, selfishness, irreligion, and ignorance. The home front is under siege. This peril is a call to action. Fathers and mothers must awake to their God-given privilege and responsibility. Churches must grasp their supreme opportunity to help parents build virile Christian homes. The Sunday School Board senses its obligation to provide materials that will generate Christian faith and Christian family living. *Home Life* is the means for launching a united movement to strengthen and enrich the home life of Southern Baptists.[1]

In a sense, Southern Baptist concern for the family has changed little since 1947. Indeed, *Home Life* remains an important resource for addressing family issues within America's largest Protestant denomination. At the same time, significant transitions in Southern and American culture, as well as in the denomination itself, have impacted the Convention's response to family matters. This brief study surveys Southern Baptist attitudes toward the family during the last five decades. It suggests that whereas significant attention has been given to the nature of family life, the denomination continues to struggle with ways of confronting family problems. Likewise, SBC leaders are often divided over the meaning of the family, as well as ways to aid its stability and growth.

Southern Baptist Distinctives

Historically, the Southern Baptist Convention exists within that segment of the Free Church tradition originating with a band of seventeenth-century English Separatists exiled in Amsterdam. By 1608, they accepted believer's baptism as normative for the church. Returning to England in 1612, these General (Arminian) Baptists became fearless advocates of religious liberty. During the 1630s, Puritanism gave birth to yet another Baptist group, this one known as Particular Baptists because of their Calvinist views.

In 1639, Roger Williams founded the first Baptist church in the American colonies in Providence, Rhode Island. Williams and other colonial Baptists challenged religious establishments in New England and the South, promoting religious liberty for believer and unbeliever alike. Strong supporters of the patriot cause, Baptists flourished in the post-Revolutionary era. In 1814 they formed their first national organization, the Triennial Convention, to facilitate the missionary enterprise. A Home Mission Society began in 1832. Each society was autonomous, supported directly by individuals and congregations. By the 1830s, Baptists were second only to Methodists among America's largest denominations.

The SBC was formed in 1845 as a result of a schism over the question of slavery and the refusal of the mission board to appoint slaveholding missionaries. Southern Baptists organized around a more connectional convention system with more closely linked agencies and boards than in the former society method.

Southern Baptists generally share certain distinctive characteristics with other Baptist bodies: (1) the authority of Holy Scripture and the liberty of the individual conscience; (2) a regenerate church membership that observes the ordinances of immersion Baptism and the Lord's Supper; (3) the autonomy of the local congregation and associational cooperation; (4) concern for an ordained clergy and the priesthood of the laity; (5) evangelistic and missionary zeal; and (6) support of religious liberty.

Southern Baptist theology reflects influences drawn from Calvinism, Arminianism, and Landmarkism (a nineteenth-century movement claiming to trace Baptist churches directly back to Jesus' baptism by John the Baptist). More recently, divisions have occurred between SBC fundamentalists and moderates over control of the convention and the role certain dogmas such as biblical inerrancy play in denominational life. As

the twentieth century comes to a close, the corporate identity and organizational structure of the SBC is becoming increasingly fragmented.[2]

Throughout much of SBC history, issues of theology, polity, preaching, and response to family were shaped significantly by its location in
the American South. Some have suggested that the SBC became the
"Catholic Church of the South," establishing hegemony over the religious life of the region.[3] The links between the Convention and Southern culture were so strong that historian John Lee Eighmy could describe the SBC as an example of "churches in cultural captivity." So
intricately woven was the religious and the regional ethos that it was often impossible to distinguish "Southernness" from "Southern Baptist-
ness."[4] Historian Samuel Hill, Jr., observed that "the religion of the
Southern People and their culture have been linked by the tightest
bonds. That culture, particularly in its moral aspects, could not have
survived without a legitimating impetus provided by religion. . . . For
the South to stand its people had to be religious and its churches the
purest anywhere."[5] Thus attitudes toward the family were influenced by
both the Southern and the Baptist elements of the Convention.

The role of the family has been an intricate part of the religious and
cultural mythology of the SBC. Southern Baptists have long viewed the
family as an extension of the church, nurturing children in faith, promoting Christian values, and witnessing to the power of grace in the
community. This basic response to the nature of the family has not
changed greatly since the 1940s. In fact, Southern Baptists have intensified their efforts to support the family even as they mourn the changing
structures of contemporary family life. As in other segments of society,
diagnoses of and prescriptions for responding to problems in family
structures often created divisions among Southern Baptists themselves.

Southern Baptists
in the Postwar Era

Southern Baptist concern for the family and its place in Christian civilization increased dramatically in the twentieth century with a corre-
sponding increase in denominational programs and publications. Family ministry was so important that multiple denominational agencies
were encouraged to focus on it. In 1941, for example, the Convention
established Christian Home Week. The denomination's Training Union
Department provided churches with teaching materials focusing on the
family.[6] By the 1960s, the Christian Life Commission, an agency that

concentrated on ethical issues, began sponsoring conferences on marriage and family life. These forums dealt with such issues as divorce, sex education, women's roles, and parenting.[7] In 1946, the Convention's Sunday School Board began the publication of *Home: A Magazine for the Christian Family.* A year later it became *Home Life,* a magazine that continues to be a significant vehicle for cultivating family and church cooperation.

The first edition of *Home Life* introduced a series of articles by Baptist ethicist T. B. Maston, titled "What's Happening to Our Homes?" These articles defined the nature of the family from a biblical and a Southern Baptist perspective. Maston noted that although the American family was always changing, "the present period" was marked by particular transition. His definition of the Christian family of that era doubtless would appeal to most Southern Baptists today. It stated that:

> God's plan and purpose for the home includes at least the following: one man and one woman joining together in holy union for life; this is to be a union of intimate, understanding fellowship; this union, with the co-operation of God, is to result in the creation of new life; the home is to be a fellowship of love that inspires the members of the family to give themselves unselfishly to the promotion of the cause of Christ among men.[8]

Maston's *Home Life* articles, like others that followed, warned of the threats to the stability of American families. He noted, for example, that the number of divorces had increased from 10,000 in 1867 to 264,000 in 1940, and insisted that the upheavals and separations of the war years had exacerbated the problem.[9]

Maston was not alone in his concern about the breakdown of family life in the postwar era. *Home Life* editor Joe Burton wrote

> The prevailing breakdown of the home cannot continue. Society is on an icy toboggan and will simply destroy itself. People must come to their senses. They must bring a spiritual factor into home life. Family living must be stabilized or else civilization is doomed. The threat of atomic destruction is insignificant in comparison with the destructive, explosive spirit of failure in home life. It cannot go on. . . . We are in a crusade. . . . Our purpose is to build Christian homes—the healthy family environment which our children need.[10]

Since then, Southern Baptists have promoted certain Christian family ideals: (1) nurturing children to faith and instructing them in moral and spiritual living; (2) worshiping in both the church and the home;

(3) cultivating Christian attitudes and actions in family relationships; and (4) actively responding to the challenges produced by the broader ("worldly") culture. Church and home thus form an alliance for the benefit not only of individuals and families but also, ultimately, of society as a whole.

While these attitudes were not unique to religious movements in the South, they reflect a particular intensity in the region. As Hill wrote in 1966, "A paramount feature in the unusual meaning the church has held for Southerners is the intensity and vitality which is its hallmark almost everywhere. . . . Popular southern religion is anything but casual about either its business or its self-identity."[11] That intensity is most evident in Southern Baptist responses to the family.

Home and Church in Partnership

Concern for a partnership between home and church is evident in many SBC agencies during the last half century. A 1971 article in *Church Training* magazine declared: "It is becoming apparent to both church leaders and parents that most of our efforts in Christian education produce only nominal results. . . .We must therfor [sic] be willing to accept the fact that the home, not the church, has to be the primary Christian educator of our children. This situation demands reorientation for both church leaders and parents."[12] The author noted that Christian education at home "does not consist simply of prayer, Bible reading, and strict attendance at all functions of the church." Rather, home was "a laboratory of unique qualities where learning takes place." It involved teaching by example and "verbal teaching of religious concepts. . . . In many instances when the home does not produce basic Christian education, the efforts of the church produce only token results."[13]

For the last fifty years, Southern Baptists have insisted that a vital aspect of Christian parenting involves the religious instruction of children. Of particular import was the need to bring all children to conversion, a "saving knowledge of Jesus Christ." Baptist insistence on a believer's church meant that baptism was deferred until individuals could make a "decision for Christ," accepting God's grace for themselves. Although Baptists used the language of conversion to describe salvation as an immediate, dramatic event, extensive emphasis also has been given to the role of the family in nurturing children to faith. Children reared in Southern Baptist homes were more likely to be baptized in the elementary years, certainly by early adolescence.[14] Families were encouraged to cultivate faith within their children, utilizing the services of the church in worship, Sunday School, Training Union (Sunday evenings), Vacation Bible School, special groups for boys and girls, and, eventually, Baptist colleges.[15]

Likewise, Christian parents were urged to lead their children to Christ. As one writer noted: "The parent has no happier privilege than to take his children on his knees to teach them of the blessed Saviour. The alert Christian father and mother will begin early, just as soon as the children can understand, telling them of the blessed Saviour and his never-ending, all transcending love."[16] Parents themselves were to model Christian virtue. Thus,

> whisky drinking, honky-tonks, gambling, horse racing, murder, robbery and debauchery of every kind are all bound up in the same bundle. To be for one is to be for all. . . . We must have Christian homes, and to have Christian homes we must lead our children to Christ. In so doing Christian parents will experience the happiest moments of their lives. Let us pledge ourselves that we will win our own to the Saviour.[17]

Family worship was another important SBC focus. Convention programs encouraged family altars—specific gatherings of the family for prayer and Bible study. From its beginning, *Home Life* magazine provided a section titled "Altar Fires," monthly Bible readings "recommended for Daily Worship in the Home." These family devotions continue to be published in numerous Baptist periodicals today. Family worship was today nonnegotiable. In 1947, Norman Cox wrote: "Experience proves that the primary source of religious character growth is the home and family. No church, nation, or civilization ever rises higher than the spirit of religious reverence and worship that prevails in the home life of its people."[18]

The following verses titled "The Altar" reflect both the piety and mythology of the Christian family in SBC life:

> I knew a simple altar
> When I was very young,
> Where quiet prayers were offered
> And sacred songs were sung.
>
> We made a little circle,
> A lovely thing to see,
> When both my dad and mother
> Knelt with the family.

A strength was wrought within me
In moments such as those;
To me a gift was given
That only heaven knows.

And in my inner being
Foundations deep were laid,
While evening after evening
My dad and mother prayed.[19]

When "dad and mother prayed" with their children they were fulfilling an important element of their calling as Christian parents. For years (and to some extent today), the model Southern Baptist family involved a father who worked and a mother who stayed at home to nurture children. In 1950, Baptist family specialist J. Clark Hensley observed that Southern Baptists reflected varying ideals for parenting. These included the "traditional model" involving an "authoritarian, hierarchical, parent-centered/parent controlled" approach and a more contemporary approach that was "authoritative but democratic, person-centered, [and] mutually submissive."[20]

The Changing Role of Women

Parenting models were particularly evident in the changing role of women. Even in the 1940s, evidence of change was underway. A 1947 *Home Life* article titled "Elizabeth Montgomery, Career Mother," noted that "marriage, motherhood, and a career can sometimes be combined successfully, believes Mrs. Montgomery; her own example is a notable case in point."[21] Montgomery put her husband and two children "first," yet also developed a career as author of "semitechnical books for teenagers." "For her, marriage and motherhood and a career mix beautifully and each is a vital ingredient of a wonderful blend she calls happiness."[22]

Denominational periodicals of the 1960s reflect other dilemmas that confronted families, particularly women. For example, in a *Home Life* article, "Can I Control Birth?" a young mother acknowledged her uncertainty as to the appropriate moral and biblical response to birth control. Though admitting she has indeed "lived under the influence of birth control" herself (that is, practiced it), she reports that she is again pregnant and, she says, "I am convinced that babies are a blessing and a reward from God. . . . And I ask in amazement, 'How could I "control" such a blessing as this?' "[23]

Women's employment outside the home has long been a subject of debate among Southern Baptists. One *Home Life* issue sought to present both sides of the question in two distinct articles. In an article titled, "Going to Work Was Good for Me," presented as "A mother's testimony about some of the personal benefits of employment outside the home," the author noted: "On the job, I came to realize how very practical the teachings of Jesus Christ are for daily life in our present time."[24] She also offered a spiritual rationale for women working outside the home: it increased the family tithe to the church. She wrote

> the tithe of working women really adds up to quite a contribution; my pastor says it would be a bad day for the churches if all the tithing women suddenly lost their jobs! . . . The services of my church refreshed and revitalized me. I went to church wearily but came away relaxed and ready for the week ahead. . . . Identifying with other working women in our church—and more than half were employed—I developed a new respect for them.[25]

This article was followed by one that presented the other side. Titled "The Job That Didn't Work," it began: "She learned that a job for the wife is not always the answer to a family's financial ills."[26] In this case, financial and personal complications led the author to relinquish her job and return to the home.

Divorce and Remarriage

The question of the role of women in the home was only one of many family crises that Southern Baptists were often slow to confront. One analyst of SBC actions comments that "Rather than being initiators in dealing with alternative patterns of family, Southern Baptists most often have *reacted to* patterns forming. Literature production, rather than being used preventively, often followed after problem areas arose."[27] Baptists tended to maintain particular dogmas regarding the ideal family until the realities of family life forced them to deal with specific problems.

This was particularly evident in the issue of divorce. For years Southern Baptists approached divorce as an unacceptable alternative for married couples. Convention resolutions in 1885 and 1904 affirmed that divorce was only acceptable for the "scriptural grounds" of adultery (Matt. 19:9) and urged ministers not to perform the remarriage of divorced persons.[28] A 1975 resolution noted that many people "turn to

divorce as an early solution" when other responses could be made that
might save the marriage. It urged "churches not only to proclaim that
monogamy is Christ's teaching for marriage but also to provide com-
passionate help for couples who face marital problems."[29]

Divorce has been a serious issue for Southern Baptist families and
churches. The question of the church's sanction of remarriage remains
divisive, though less so today among both clergy and laity. Likewise,
Southern Baptists are divided over the role of divorced people in the
church and whether they should be permitted to serve as pastors, dea-
cons, teachers, or in other leadership capacities. By the 1980s, Southern
Baptists were forced to acknowledge the widespread divorce rate within
their ranks, even among denominational and congregational leaders.

Remarriage itself, even after the death of a mate, was a serious enough
question for a 1976 *Home Life* article on the subject. The authors, who
had remarried after having lost spouses, assured readers that scripture
indicated that "relationships in heaven are spiritual. . . . We shall be
brothers and sisters in Christ and be as angels."[30] Apparently, some in
the churches were uncertain whether Christians could remarry when a
spouse died.

Broadening Themes
in Southern Baptist Family Life

Gradually, Southern Baptists came to recognize the changing dynamics of family life. This became evident in various articles on the difficulties and struggles confronting even the Christian family. For example, a 1976 item in *Home Life* dealt with the difficulties of parenting
problem children, particularly poignant during the "counter-culture"
generation of that era. Subtitled "Should Parents Blame Themselves
When Their Children Go Wrong?" it is accompanied by a photograph
showing a bearded youth being arrested by police. The author observes:

> Many of today's youth shun parents because they feel that the older
> generation is too materialistic. They want to build a different
> world. . . . Some sincerely believe in health foods, exercise, and
> vegetarianism. Who are we to judge whether they are right or
> wrong? . . . If your child wanders off the path, don't blame your-
> self as a parent. Hope and pray that someday your child will see
> the error of his ways. In the meantime, continue to give him your
> love and support without robbing him of the chance to learn his
> lessons by himself.[31]

That article, written in 1976, reflects a broadening of themes relative to families in the 1970s and 1980s. Increasing attention was given to such topics as parenting children with special needs, the importance of the extended family, caring for foster children, and the complexity of family relationships. For example, a 1972 *Church Training* article suggested, "This is certainly a new day for the mentally retarded and their families. We have moved from smuggling the mentally retarded into the back doors of churches to walking with them through the front doors."[32] Churches were urged to respond to the continuing needs of families where persons with disabilities were present.

As Baptists confronted the realities of the changing world around them, they were particularly concerned about the impact of the use of alcohol on the family. Across the last several decades, SBC publications have targeted liquor use and sales as major social and family problems. In a 1956 article, C. Aubrey Hearn warned that "beer is served in the homes of more than two thirds of the forty million families in the United States."[33] He urged parents to boycott stores that sold beer and to write letters against beer advertising to companies and television networks. However, "the best solution is the increasing devotion of the members of the family to the principles of the Bible, to purposeful activity in various meetings and organizations of the church, and to the projection of Christian ideals in everyday living."[34]

Family Issues in Recent Baptist Battles

A recent fundamentalist resurgence in the SBC has changed the focus of family issues. For example, during the last twenty years the SBC has passed resolutions that, among other things, deplore the "Children's Rights Movement," affirm that "man" is "the head of the woman" in "God's order of authority for his church and the Christian home," and support legislation or a constitutional amendment "prohibiting abortion except to save the life of the mother."[35] A 1980 resolution deplored and rejected the "homosexual lifestyle," and any effort to make "it equally acceptable to the biblical heterosexual family life style."[36] Other recent developments include a major denominational campaign called "True Love Waits," an attempt to promote virginity until marriage for both males and females.[37] The program, which has attracted wide attention in the secular media, encourages teenagers to pledge themselves to maintain chastity as long as they are unmarried. Likewise, the SBC continues to promote "Fall Festivals of Marriage," a series of workshops held throughout the country. Leaders claimed that some 2,300 couples were involved in six retreats in 1990 alone.[38] During the last two to three decades, local churches have become more intentional about their work with families. This is evident in the increase in marriage enrichment retreats, divorce recovery workshops, and even the construction of "family life centers" that provide varying sports and exercise programs for family members both young and old.

Given recent disputes in convention life, some suggest that the fundamentalist (conservative) dominance of denominational life has contributed to the influence of more authoritarian approaches to family life and ministry evident in the ideas and programs of conservative Christian psychologist James Dobson and seminar leader Bill Gothard. Gothard's "Chain of Command" describes God's plan for family authority with the father as "head" under Christ, and with women and children under that authority.[39] Likewise, many local churches have used books and videos from Dobson as resources for focusing on the family.

Debates continue among fundamentalist and moderate Southern Baptists over the nature of women's role in both family and church, with many fundamentalists pressing for various forms of "submission" and many moderates promoting a more egalitarian response. Recently, SBC agencies, particularly the Christian Life Commission, have attacked the media and social issues, such as homosexuality and abortion, that they believe undermine traditional family values.

Conclusions are as follows: First, Southern Baptist views on the family remain those of a conservative, evangelical people. Baptists generally continue to insist that the biblical model for the family involves one man and one woman who are married and faithful to each other and rear their children in ways that model, nurture, and inculcate Christian faith and morals. Second, for the last half century the SBC has used its denominational resources and system to provide encouragement and instruction for families. Through a wide variety of Convention programs and publications, Southern Baptists have attempted to promote the importance of the Christian family and to respond to its needs. Third, Southern Baptist response to certain transitions in American family life has changed significantly over the last fifty years, albeit slowly and not without struggle. This is particularly evident in the issue of divorce and the dramatic rise in single-family households during the last several decades. Indeed, Baptists have struggled both to maintain and promote their ideal for the family while developing new family ministries in response to the inescapable realities of contemporary family life. Efforts to come to terms with those realities are particularly evident in denominational materials produced during the 1970s and early 1980s. Finally, during the last eight to ten years changes in the leadership of the denomination have facilitated the conservative emphases of programs for families. These include a strong opposition to almost all types of abortion and to homosexuality, promotion of sexual abstinence until marriage, and other programs associated with what is often termed "traditional family values."

It is clear that Southern Baptists, regardless of their theological orientation, remain concerned about the family and the church's response to family issues. Moving toward the new millennium, Baptists no doubt will continue to promote certain ideals for the Christian family while struggling to respond to the ever-changing realities of American family life.

NOTES

1. Clifton J. Allen, "Our Utmost for the Highest," *Home Life* (January 1947):1.
2. Bill J. Leonard, *God's Last and Only Hope: The Fragmentation of the Southern Baptist Convention* (Grand Rapids: Wm. B. Eerdmans Publ. Co., 1990); and Nancy Ammerman, *Baptist Battles* (New York: Rutgers University Press, 1990).
3. Leonard, *God's Last and Only Hope.*
4. John Lee Eighmy, *Churches in Cultural Captivity* (Knoxville: University of Tennessee Press, 1976); and Charles Reagan Wilson, *Baptized in Blood, the Religion of the Lost Cause, 1865–1920* (Athens: University of Georgia Press, 1980).
5. Samuel Hill, Jr., *Religion and the Solid South* (Nashville: Abingdon Press, 1972), 36.
6. G. Wade Rowatt and Dianne Bertolino-Green, "Family Ministries among Southern Baptists," *Baptist History and Heritage* (January 1982):14; and Phillip B. Harris, "Help Available for the Family," *Church Training* (April 1972):4.
7. J. Clark Hensley, "Trends in Baptist Family Life," *Baptist History and Heritage* (January 1982):10–12.
8. T. B. Maston, "What's Happening to Our Homes?" *Home Life* (January 1946):6.
9. Ibid., 7.
10. Joe Burton, "A Crusade for Christian Homes," *Home Life* (July 1947):3.
11. Samuel Hill, Jr., *Southern Churches in Crisis* (Boston: Beacon Press, 1966), 164.
12. J. David Prewitt, "The Role of the Home in Christian Education," *Church Training* (December 1971):22.

13. Ibid.
14. Bill J. Leonard, "Southern Baptists and Conversion: An Evangelical Sacramentalism," in *Ties That Bind: Life Together in the Baptist Vision,* ed. Gary A. Furr and Curtis W. Freeman (Macon, Ga.: Smyth & Helwys Publishers, 1994).
15. Mrs Edwin S. Preston, "Teaching Our Children about God," *Home Life* (January 1947):16–17.
16. Bruce Twitty, "Leading Our Children to Christ," *Home Life* (January 1947):30.
17. Ibid., 31. See also Mrs. C. A. Hearn, and Myrtle O. Looney, "Learning at Home," *Home Life* (February 1956):47; and Fred Lackey, "God's Revelation for the Family," *Alabama Baptist* (28 January 1988):3.
18. Norman Cox, "Why Have Family Worship?" *Home Life* (May 1947):21.
19. Lon Woodrum, "The Altar," *Home Life* (February 1956):21.
20. Hensley, "Trends in Baptist Family Life," 11.
21. Nancy Vogel, "Elizabeth Montgomery: Career Mother," *Home Life* (April 1947):6–7.
22. Ibid., 6.
23. Pat Sims, "Can I Control Birth?" *Home Life* (January 1968):11.
24. Martha Nelson, "Going to Work Was Good for Me," *Home Life* (December 1975):24–25.
25. Ibid.
26. Charlene Taylor, "The Job That Didn't Work," *Home Life* (December 1975):26–27. The debate on this subject continues, see Cyndi Allison Wittum, "I Can't Afford NOT to Stay Home," *Home Life* (March 1994).
27. William M. Tillman, Jr., "Patterns in Family Ethics in Baptist Life," *Baptist History and Heritage* (January 1982):35.
28. Southern Baptist Convention, *Annual* (1885):30–31; Southern Baptist Convention, *Annual* (1904):46; and Reuben Herring, "Southern Baptist Convention Resolutions on the Family," *Baptist History and Heritage* (January 1982):40.
29. Southern Baptist Convention, *Annual* (1975):74; and Herring, "Southern Baptist Convention Resolutions on the Family," 41.
30. Robert and Ann McCoy Scales, "Remarriage after the Death of a Mate," *Home Life* (May 1976):46–48.
31. Phyllis Gilbert, "Playing the Blame Game," *Home Life* (March 1976):16–17.
32. Bobby Perry, "Visiting with Parents of the Mentally Retarded," *Church Training* (April 1972):42–43. See also Alice Bostrom, "Foster Child," *Home Life* (March 1976):40–41; Thomas W. Klewin, "Wanted: Relatives," *Home Life* (May 1976):42–43; and "We Love Inker-Winker," *Home Life* (July 1976):6–7.
33. C. Aubrey Hearn, "Is TV Making Beer Drinkers of Our Children?" *Home Life* (April 1956):8–9.
34. Ibid. See also Thomas B. McDormand, "Why Christians Are Total Abstain-

ers," *Home Life* (September 1956):8–9; Sam Morris, "Liquor Advertising and Juvenile Delinquency," *Home Life* (October 1956):10–12; and Margaret A. Lane, "The Alcoholic: How Dependable His Glass Crutch?" *Home Life* (December 1968):15–17.

35. Southern Baptist Convention, *Annual* (1980):55–56; Southern Baptist Convention, *Annual* (1973):87; Southern Baptist Convention, *Annual* (1980): 48–49; and Herring, "Southern Baptist Convention Resolutions on the Family," 38–39, 43.

36. Southern Baptist Convention, *Annual* (1980):55; and Herring, "Southern Baptist Convention Resolutions on the Family," 50.

37. Trennis Henderson, "True Love Waits—A Parable," *Home Life* (November 1994):3. See also "True Love Waits Rally," *Home Life* (July 1994):19.

38. James H. Cox, "A Fall Festival Reaffirmed Our Love," *Home Life* (August 1990):29.

39. Hensley, "Trends in Baptist Family Life," 9–10; and Guy Greenfield, "Today's Christian Man," *Home Life* (June 1994):21–23.

2

Latter-day Saints:
Home Can Be a
Heaven on Earth

CLAUDIA L. BUSHMAN WITH
RICHARD L. BUSHMAN

In 1947, I traveled from California to Utah with my family for the "Days of '47" celebration of 100 years of Latter-day Saint life in the Salt Lake Valley. My family joined thousands of others in flocking to that valley to attend celebratory parades and dedicatory ceremonies. The events commemorated the arrival of Brigham Young and his wagon train of Mormon pioneers from Missouri in 1847. Rising from a sick bed and gazing over the arid salt flats, he had exclaimed, "This is the place, drive on!"

The Mormon story had begun over a decade earlier, when an angel appeared to a farm boy in upstate New York and arranged for him to dig up Golden Plates that were translated to be the Book of Mormon, a witness for Jesus Christ on the American continents. That eastern chapter of the story ended tragically with Joseph Smith's murder after he and his followers had moved to Illinois. The arrival of the first pioneers in the Utah valley of the Great Salt Lake (the world's largest organized overland migration), and the territory building, which made the wilderness blossom like the rose, began the Mormon Church's western myth.

Going to Salt Lake for the "Days of '47" was a major event for my family, second- and third-generation Latter-day Saints. Both sides of my family had moved to California in the twenties. Unlike the original settlers, we traveled to the Salt Lake Valley from the other direction, and we stayed at the elegant Hotel Utah, the Edwardian hostelry across the street from Temple Square, not a pioneer cabin. We came in style to the Utah our families had left in poverty a generation before.

Although they left Zion, our family members had remained faithful, committed, and active Mormons. They prospered in California and were able to provide social and educational advantages for their children, becoming cosmopolitan San Franciscans. But they also stayed committed to the Mormon cause and spent many hours a week at the Mormon church. Our family believed in Joseph Smith's exotic visions and revelations, as well as the continuation of living prophets, and we did not smoke or drink, not even tea or coffee. However, we moved easily among our Baptist, Roman Catholic, and Presbyterian neighbors. Although we were Californians we were also Mormons, and we were charmed and thrilled to participate in events where Mormons commemorated a proud pioneer past.

Latter-day Saints, Family Life, and American Culture

Following World War II, perhaps for the first time in their history, Latter-day Saints reflected the widespread cultural values of the majority of citizens. This was a happy circumstance for a church that had begun as a maverick sect and had suffered persecution for its beliefs, its members ridiculed and driven until they reached the Salt Lake Valley. Although Mormons hoped to be left alone in Utah, they were persecuted even there by the United States government, which would not tolerate Latter-day Saint idiosyncracies. Utah gained statehood only after forswearing the distinctive form of Mormon plural marriage. After 1900, by stressing education, hard work, and self-sufficiency, the Mormons began to achieve social and financial strength. The post–World War II period capped half a century of accommodation to American values. In postwar America, when "the family that pray[ed] together, stay[ed] together," Mormons lived in harmony with and echoed major social trends. The church, with its century of conservative agrarian history, embraced the return to the hearth, resonating with prevailing popular values.

A consideration of the family after World War II is an intriguing subject for a Mormon. Since the war, the church has changed both dramatically and not very much. The membership of the church has increased eight times since 1945,[1] expanding around the world. But with a new and enlarged cast of characters, the church is still recognizably the same old-fashioned, revelation-respecting, family-oriented, tradition-valuing group of proselytizing Christians.

Although family life has always been central to the Church of Jesus Christ of Latter-day Saints, after 1945 popular interest encouraged the church to emphasize family issues. Both the members and the church leadership began teaching in church meetings the primacy of the family as never before. A favorite and much-quoted teaching of church president David O. McKay was "No other success can compensate for failure in the home."[2] The phrase, honored and quoted since the forties, is shorthand for the idea that maintaining strong family relationships must come before the concerns of school, work, community, and even the church. Harold B. Lee, a later church president, underlined this idea by saying, "The most important of the Lord's work [you] will ever do will be the work you do within the walls of your own homes."[3]

In adapting this approach for missionary work, attractive Mormon families were used as evidence for the truthfulness of Mormon doctrines. Short-haired and clean-cut, the missionaries themselves reflected wholesome American family life. The importance of the family was written into the missionary lessons, along with the hope that converts would achieve the happy families pictured in the American dream.

The church in many ways appropriated American family values. The family became the focus of public relations. The "Homefront" television advertisements presented the church as wise and sensitive in personal relations, supporting the verities of kindness, helpfulness, and harmonious communities. The Tabernacle Choir represented the people next door joined in song. The church sought to portray mainstream America in representations of itself to the public.

During this period, a number of basic programs were reclassified to emphasize the importance of family life. The *Home Night* program, which set aside Monday evenings for family activities and scriptural study, had been around since the Depression. Begun to strengthen and improve the family, Home Night was credited with much of the unity and strength for which the Mormons have been known. To reassert its continuing importance, Home Night was renamed *Family Home Evening;* the stress was put on the *people* who gathered rather than the *place.* Extensive manuals were prepared to help families teach gospel living in the home. Participants were promised that regular Family Home Evening participation would develop increased personal worth and family unity. "Love at home and obedience to parents will increase, and faith will develop in the hearts of the youth."[4] For emphasis, other church programs were retitled and capitalized: Family Prayer, Family Scripture Study, and Family Worship. The social programs of the church were praised, admired, and emulated. Latter-day Saints were definitely at the forefront of family values, in both practice and promotion.

For obvious reasons, church members were alarmed when the social values of American society subsequently swung to the left. There had always been a counterculture, but in the late 1960s traditional values were questioned as never before; dubious moral behavior became widespread. What had been a counterculture became a powerful popular culture. Women questioned customary roles as servants to the house and family and demanded recognition as individuals. A new awareness of ecology persuaded influential scientists that having many children was unwise. Traditional family values became increasingly marginalized as movies, television, and pop music seemed to glamorize sexual immorality.

Latter-day Saints nevertheless held tight to their traditional values during the difficult sixties and seventies, feeling virtuous and embattled, and expecting reason to return. But when the smoke cleared, a new world was revealed. While a majority of the population probably maintained traditional, even conservative views, the media espoused more liberal ones. Moreover, the sexual revolution had loosened the structure of traditional morality, leading to a rise in divorce and births outside of marriage. The brief convergence of Mormon with American values was rudely halted. A new public culture undermined the family priorities that Mormons treasured and had made preeminently their own.

Latter-day Saint Family Theology

Many churches adjusted to the changing times, but the Church of Jesus Christ of Latter-day Saints did not. Mormon theology prevents believers from shifting their positions. The *Mormon Plan of Salvation* lays out a map of individual existence, charting progress from premortal life, through time on earth, and on to life after resurrection. The plan teaches us that we live in a family before birth, as spirit children of our Heavenly Father; that we create families on earth—our most important purpose in this life; and that we preserve our families for future life. The *family* is central and eternal. Marriage and procreation are primary and children are welcomed. The marriage bond is permanent and exclusive. Couples are married for "time and all eternity," and their children are "sealed" to them forever.

Individuals are linked together as married couples and as families in Mormon temples that are used predominantly for the ordinances and ceremonies that unite families all over the world. There were eight of these temples after World War II; now some fifty temples are accessible to believers.

The temple ceremonies and ordinances—called baptisms, endowments, and sealings—connect living families, but the ancestral link is also important. Church members also help non-Mormon families who are interested in their ancestors and family genealogy. The church's extensive Family History program copies genealogical records from around the world and stores them on microfilm in a central library in Salt Lake City, supporting individual genealogical research for temple work. Copies of these records can be sent to local Family History Centers worldwide. Mormons are encouraged to search the records for their ancestors and to perform temple ordinances for them. This complex program of genealogical records and temples exists so that Mormons can connect themselves over time into one grand Mormon family. Genealogy and temple work have a regular place in Mormon schedules. In 1945, a family might go once a year to the Salt Lake Temple. Now many thousands go weekly to local temples, testifying to the importance of the family in Mormon theology. These doctrines and practices help to erect a wall between the Church of Jesus Christ of Latter-day Saints and the current cultural deterioration of family values.

In order to teach children the basic concepts of religious life, Mormons have domesticated (a good family idiom) extramortal existence, both pre- and postmortal life, making it the same as life on earth. The popular catch phrase is "Families Are Forever." Children are taught that God is their real father and that prayers in their own words are heard and answered. Thus children are linked with their earthly biological parents in lines that connect them back to their Heavenly Father. The extramortal understanding of family is made clear in the lyrics from a popular mormon song:

> I am a child of God,
> And He has sent me here,
> Has given me an earthly home
> With parents kind and dear.
>
> Chorus
> Lead me, guide me, walk beside me,
> Help me find the way.
> Teach me all that I must do
> To live with Him someday.[5]

Reality extends beyond an earthlife to the primary relationship with deity. Children are taught to lead lives worthy of eternal salvation so they can return to the presence of God. Earthlife is only a link in the chain of conscious existence that extends before and beyond. The mission to work out an individual salvation on earth precedes allegiance to earthly parents who provide shelter and love. The song requests the help of teachers in fulfilling each person's cosmic role.

A similar message that stresses the continuation of the earth family can be seen in the song, "Families Can Be Together Forever."

> I have a fam'ly here on earth.
> They are so good to me.
> I want to share my life with them
> Through all eternity.
>
> Chorus
> Fam'lies can be together forever
> Through Heav'nly Father's plan.
> I always want to be with my own family,
> And the Lord has shown me how I can.
> The Lord has shown me how I can.
>
> While I am in my early years,
> I'll prepare most carefully,
> So I can marry in God's temple
> For eternity.[6]

Again, cosmic ideas are reduced to simple language. Children are taught that their familiar family life will continue after death, that family life must be worthy of eternal maintenance, and that the teachings of the church—particularly chastity, morality, and temple marriage—must be followed. Mormon visions of the hereafter do not reflect thrones, pearly gates, clouds, and harps. Instead, the images are more likely to be of nuclear families gathered around kitchen tables, kneeling in prayer, or dressed in crisp finery for church. Mormons of all ages are taught thus. The proper behavior for children, adolescents, and adults is repeatedly and dramatically laid out in a Plan of Salvation in which the preservation of family life is absolutely essential. Following these teachings requires delayed gratification, sacrifice, obedience, and submission, characteristics that go against the grain of current cultural ideas.

Latter-day Saint Family Life in Practice

How well does the church succeed in teaching these difficult messages to their people? I conducted a survey on family attitudes among active church members from two congregations in the eastern United States.[7] Of the thirty-nine people who responded to my survey, 90 percent believed that marriages were to be lifelong or eternal commitments, broken only after the most serious effort to reconcile differences; 68 percent would choose the same spouse again if given the chance, two-thirds of them "definitely" and one-third "probably," an indication that they all conformed to the Mormon teachings. Believing that it was their responsibility to build successful families, 64 percent defined themselves as "happy" in their family relations, 33 percent considered themselves "extraordinarily happy." The respondents not only feel that they *should* be happy, they have constructed lives and relationships that *make* them happy.

Fairly recent data from more professional studies show that more Latter-day Saints will marry, marry earlier, marry within the Mormon faith, have a lower divorce rate, and remarry after divorce than the general population.[8] Marital fidelity is honored. In my sample, all but one person said that sexual intercourse between unmarried partners was never justified. Divorce has always been permitted among Mormons and, despite teachings against it, the overall rate among all Mormons is only slightly below the national average. However, statistics show that those married in the temple divorce at a rate one-sixth that of those not married in the temple.[9]

Latter-day Saints are known for having large families. Utah, with its high percentage of Mormons (about 70 percent), boasts the highest fertility rate in the nation. However, not all Mormon families are large, and the Mormon birthrate tends to follow the peaks and valleys of the national averages. My survey included several mothers who had given birth five or more times, but the average household size was 2.8 children. Mormons will use birth control, but not as soon or as frequently as other groups.[10] Studies of the general population have shown that large family size can lead to coercive discipline and even patterns of abuse in some cases. A study of relationships among Mormons with large families has shown the opposite pattern—closer family relationships in larger families.[11] Church classes teach "inductive parenting" or "reason-oriented parenting" rather than authoritarian styles.[12] Mormons are not immune to instances of abuse both in family situations and in congregations, but admit to them and condemn them.

Latter-day Saints consistently report lower rates of premarital sexual experience, teenage pregnancy, and extramarital sexual experience than the national average.[13] A study comparing data from 1950 and 1972 reported no premarital sexual activity in more than 95 percent of respondents in groups of young adults active in the church. As expected, however, those inactive in religious life demonstrated more liberal sexual behavior.[14] The rate of teenage childbirth and illegitimacy in these situations is fairly high, with young women being encouraged to bear children conceived out of wedlock and put them up for adoption. Adoptable babies are in high demand in this family-oriented culture, and abortion is strongly discouraged.

Mormons tend to be prudish on sexual matters and to be politically conservative on social issues relating to family, sex, and drugs. In spite of this, two-thirds of respondents favor sex education in schools.[15]

These studies indicate that church members uphold many of the values the church inculcates. In actual practice, the urging of church leaders for followers to attain the highest levels of behavior can inculcate feelings of guilt. Not all members consider their families to be ideal. Many who "fail to measure up" suffer from feelings of inadequacy and the real or imagined judgments of others. Parents cannot guarantee the faithfulness of their children, and young people wander from the faith. The church acknowledges many problems in family life—divorce, abuse, unmarried maternity, premarital sex, unmarried adults, abortion, homosexuality, and marriage outside the faith—and tries to provide practical help. Although present teaching reflects very high standards, it also represents some failure to achieve those standards.

Latter-day Saint Response to Cultural Change

Many have argued that the tension between the standards of the church and the practice of Mormon doctrines will, in some cases, lead to a change in the doctrines. If members are unable to achieve the high level set for them, the church inevitably must adjust to social trends and human failings. But will the church, which has gradually adopted national norms over the past fifty years, continue to do so? This is the problem that Armand Mauss, a sociologist writing on Mormonism, addresses in his recent book *The Angel and the Beehive: The Mormon Struggle with Assimilation.* Mauss argues that Mormonism will stand firm on family issues. According to Mauss, Mormons for a long time have assimilated national culture to gain acceptance, but they are now retrenching to preserve their differences. Mauss sees that following the confluence with national culture after World War II, the church subsequently pulled back to preserve its distinctiveness. A movement that goes too far toward assimilation, he notes, may completely lose its unique identity. By mid-century, he argues, Mormonism had adapted sufficiently to survive but then reverted back to an earlier style.[16]

Mauss identifies a steady retrenchment effort emanating from church leaders. Mormons, he believes, evidence a new fundamentalism characterized by beliefs in scriptural inerrancy and literalism, authoritarian leadership, and obedience to pastoral teachings. He notes that Mormons who tithe are more generous to their church than members of other churches, just as they hold a stronger belief in their church than other religionists.[17]

Mauss bases his arguments about assimilation and retrenchment on sociological models, and they are convincing. His analysis of Mormon church structure and teachings is based on a close investigation of published speeches and some statistical surveys, as well as a lifetime of observation. The church does seem to have begun to retrench to positions reminiscent of the past pro-family stance. Whether this will be the permanent position remains to be seen. We might wonder whether after a brief time the teachings of the church once again will adapt to national norms. Will there be chinks in the wall and compromises as the church tries to uphold old ways against current trends? Or will the church continue to build walls against the encroachments of the outside world? The present is problematic; what of the future?

Changing Patterns in Marriage and the Role of Women

Holding the line against American social norms requires dealing with two obvious problems—the large number of unmarried adults and the changing role of women. In this family-oriented church, one-third of the people between twenty and thirty are single, most of them never having been married. These single people do not fit neatly into the general Plan of Salvation. Earlier teachings, now seldom heard, had consigned single adults to the role of ministering angels in the life beyond, a supportive and secondary role. Now Mormons are more likely to hear that all this will be worked out in the future, allowing for marriage in the hereafter. Although changes may come, the church teachings are still clear that individuals should marry.

The role of women is also becoming problematic. As other American women move steadily into more demanding and responsible professional positions, Mormon women still often remain at home. Mormon leaders consider it advantageous and advisable for women to care for their children full time and many Mormon women do so, seeing the care of children as their highest calling. This standard of behavior was prevalent in the 1950s and 1960s, but economic difficulties have steadily eroded the desire of many mothers to remain at home with young children, forcing them to reenter the work force.

Mormon women, however, have been strongly encouraged by church leaders to stay home with their children, even with serious financial sacrifice, although recently general authorities' counsel has been judicious and tolerant of individual situations. In my sample questionnaire, however, only 18 percent of families managed the preferred ideal of a working husband and a full-time homemaker. In 46 percent of the households, both wives and husbands worked, with about half of the working wives working full time; 36 percent had diverse arrangements.

Informal discussion with some of these mothers indicated that the decision whether to work outside the home was an area of serious conflict for them. Some mothers chose to stay at home although severely straitened and economically challenged. As a group, these women wanted to obey the church leaders and be homemakers. Others took part-time employment to bring in a little added income, trying to reconcile their economic needs and their family obligations. Working mothers and homemakers both felt defensive about their decisions. No one in this conservative community was preaching the right of women to pursue chosen careers. The issue was obedience versus economic viability.

In this issue, as in others, the women listened quietly to the counsel of leaders and then made their own decisions. Doctrines taught by the national church leaders or general authorities were interpreted by local leaders to reflect local concerns. Individual members then interpreted those doctrines to suit their own particular needs.

The church's stance on the role of women in the church is not likely to change in the near future. Gender roles are markedly differentiated, with priesthood and motherhood frequently equated in sermons. While people outside the church tend to consider Mormon women as seriously oppressed, the women themselves do not feel downtrodden. Patriarchal rhetoric is often employed alongside fairly egalitarian roles in practice. My survey shows that 59 percent of the respondents considered their marriage roles to be equal or nearly equal, 20 percent considered the husband slightly dominant, 10 percent considered the wife slightly dominant, and only 12 percent considered the husband definitely dominant—the stereotypical picture of Mormon families held by outsiders. In actual practice, 59 percent considered the discussion of family problems between the spouses to be easy rather than difficult.

However, women's role in the church has become a major problem. Even as opportunities for women are escalating in America today, women in the Mormon community find their opportunities, particularly in the church, curtailed. A general simplification and homogenization of church programs has resulted in the elimination of many of the broader cultural activities that concerned women. Some "course corrections" over programming and regimentation during the 1990s pledged that reduction and simplification would allow more family time. This restructuring resulted in the elimination of many auxiliary activities for women, girls, and children. These simplified programs have also helped assimilate converts into a strange new church.

In this retrenchment, the financially autonomous Women's Relief Society, organized by Joseph Smith as a *companion* to the male priesthood, was placed firmly under the *control* of the priesthood. As a result, women within the Society have lost leadership positions as well as considerable visibility and power in the church.[18] Because all local leadership consists of unpaid recruits from the congregation, the men bear a heavy burden. Women are much freer of such responsibility than in the past.

Although women have been relieved of much of their past responsibility, a powerful group of female leaders—underutilized, skilled administrators and scriptorians who have served missions—has grown up in the church. These women are strong, even though they are traditionally obedient and deferential. They earnestly strive to do what is right. They often oppose an Equal Rights Amendment to the Constitution, and they decide against serious professional involvements. In my survey, 64 percent of women either disagreed or strongly disagreed with the statement that the United States government should pass an Equal Rights Amendment to the Constitution to guarantee equal rights between men and women. They also feel that women's best talents are needed at home. Fifty-six percent either agreed or strongly agreed that women today are neglecting their family responsibilities by seeking a full-time career outside the home. Although Mormon women are better educated, and probably as a group more competent than ever before, they still embrace homemaking as a woman's primary calling in life.

The church has also taken a pro-life, antiabortion stance, limiting acceptable abortions for church members to cases involving rape or incest, extreme deformity, or the health or survival of the mother. The respondents in my sample echoed these beliefs. They overwhelmingly opposed legal abortions for unmarried women, for women who did not want their babies, for poor women, and for mothers with deformed fetuses. Sixty-four percent would allow abortions if the mother's own health was endangered; only 33 percent if women were pregnant by rape (although in that case 46 percent were uncertain). Even though *Roe v. Wade*, which allows first trimester abortions on demand, is the law of the land, church members consider abortion for other than the above-listed drastic reasons a sin much the same as, though not equal to, murder. This generally pro-family and pro-child stance reflects the Mormon emphasis on taking responsibility for sexual behavior.

Present and Future Prospects for Change

These themes are signs of stress and an indication of a gradual evolution toward a standard international Christian worldview. But there is also evidence that the church will maintain its distinctiveness and adhere to its postwar, pro-family stance.

One reason for stability is that traditional beliefs in the importance of family persist, even when family groupings are incomplete or after their basic form has changed. Families with grown children or households of widowed spouses, though lacking members required for a traditional family, still consider themselves traditional. Those who are not part of a traditional family would choose such a life if they could. Many single individuals or partial member families yearn to join the traditional ranks. Inactive and nonobservant Mormons still believe in the teachings of the church on family, though they depart from other church practices. This is a form of inertia, but it also is a conservative brake on change.

One might assume that the dramatic expansion of the church would create a tension with the wider community that would in turn affect teachings about families. Surprisingly, this rapid extension and expansion has led to little doctrinal evolution, despite increased membership around the globe. The need to simplify documents for translation into other languages has reinforced the teachings of the church.

When the priesthood, always limited to males, was extended to males of black African descent, most church members greeted the news with joy. They had prayed many years for that extension. Church congregations that were almost completely white fifty years ago are now racially mixed, including a significant percentage of people of color— native Americans, as well as immigrants from other countries. Many congregations reflect this international membership. In every nation in which it resides, the Church of Jesus Christ of Latter-day Saints has similar meetings, reads from the same scriptures, and sings the same songs, which are translated into their own languages. Even taking cultural dissimilarities into consideration, local differences are still modest. Leaders in other nations have been called to membership in the councils of general authorities. Multiculturalism serves to simplify the gospel messages that come from the leaders of the church, but what these messages lose in specificity, they gain in power.[19]

Change is also impeded by the early indoctrination of children in church programs and at their mothers' knees. Although some women leave the home to work, those who stay behind have inordinate influence over their children's beliefs and futures. Children receive early teaching in family unity, reinforced by the Family Home Evening program. They are taught a work ethic, to seek a good education, to become responsible adults, and to save money. Leadership in the congregations provides lessons, role models, and opportunities for service. Teenagers receive an hour of "Seminary" each day before school. These programs make religious discussion an active part of daily life and bring the young people together for social purposes. An "Institute" program provides similar instructional classes and social activity for college students. In my study, an impressive 77 percent claimed participation in family or group worship at home in addition to praying over the food, which all regularly did. Family prayer, scripture study, and Family Home Evening are a basic part of home life.

The missionary program now enlists more than 50,000 young men and women.[20] Young men are strongly encouraged to go on two-year missions; many young women choose to go too. These young people—removed from college programs, professional experience, and serious romances—transfer their youthful energies to spreading the gospel, reinforcing their own beliefs in the process. While their two years of proselytizing may not be the most efficient method to convert new members for the Mormon Church, the group is so large that convert baptisms between 1986 and 1990 still outnumbered baptisms of members' children by three to one.[21]

Serving a mission is considered a climactic highpoint for a young Mormon. A very demanding and difficult experience, it nevertheless provides spiritual enlightenment, lasting friendships, and extraordinary satisfaction. Financial support for those serving missions comes mainly from the parents of the missionaries, although funds can usually be found to support those who are without savings or supportive families. As many Mormon families have multiple children and single incomes, mission work represents financial sacrifice. However, although missions are costly, they are burdens happily assumed, representing the fulfilled ambitions of fond parents. The missionary's experience focuses the attentions and resources of the whole family.

Not every missionary has a positive experience, and some do not complete the course; however, most do finish their assignments, returning home to embrace the programs the church has laid out for them—education and temple marriage, for instance.

This system has protected the church against the attacks on family values over the past two decades. Mormons have clung tenaciously to the ideal of family life that was in fashion briefly after World War II. As debates about family policy rage between the conservative and the liberal camps, Mormons today are involved only peripherally. They see themselves as upholding a divine standard against barbarians and hedonists. They are not interested in being influenced either by national governments or by other churches, believing instead that their own ways provide the best hope for the nation and the world. Mormons do not want to debate; they are already convinced that they are right in encouraging close and happy families and responsible parenthood. They see the only hope for a healthy society to be in healthy individual homes. As Harold B. Lee, a recent president of the church, said:

> It is becoming increasingly clear that the home and family are the keys to the future of the church. An unloved child, a child who has not known discipline, work, or responsibility, will often yield to Satanic substances for happiness—drugs, sexual experimentation and rebellion, whether it is intellectual or behavioral. Our intensified efforts . . . hold much promise if we but use these opportunities.[22]

As Mormons continue to march out of step with the dominant popular culture, whatever difficulties arise, they are unlikely to yield much on family values.

NOTES

1. Armand L. Mauss, *The Angel and the Beehive: The Mormon Struggle with Assimilation* (Urbana, Ill.: University of Illinois Press, 1994), 123.
2. Quoted in David O. McKay, *Family Home Evening Manual* (Salt Lake City: Church of Jesus Christ of Latter-day Saints, Council of the Twelve, 1965), iii.
3. Harold B. Lee, *Strengthening the Home* (Salt Lake City: Church of Jesus Christ of Latter-day Saints, Council of the Twelve, 1973), 7.

4. *Family Home Evening Manual* (Salt Lake City: Church of Jesus Christ of Latter-day Saints, Council of the Twelve, 1977–78), v.

5. Naomi W. Randall and Mildred T. Pettit, "I am a Child of God," *Hymns of the Church of Jesus Christ of Latter-day Saints* (Salt Lake City: The Church of Jesus Christ of Latter-day Saints, Council of the Twelve, 1985), 301. Copyright © The Church of Jesus Christ of Latter-day Saints, used by permission.

6. Ruth M. Gardner and Vanja Y. Watkins, "Families Can Be Together Forever," *Hymns*, 300. Copyright © The Church of Jesus Christ of Latter-day Saints, used by permission of publisher and author.

7. In the spring of 1994, I conducted this anonymous survey of family attitudes with two groups of active Mormon adults in Virginia, a fairly conservative Mormon area. I had thirty-nine respondents: thirty-one from a Sunday school class in Charlottesville; eight from an informal gathering of women in Richmond. The respondents included married, single, widowed, and retired individuals. Half listed household income as below $50,000 a year, with eight below the $30,000 level. Of the half above $50,000, six listed incomes over $100,000.

8. Tim B. Heaton, "Four C's of the Mormon Family: Chastity, Conjugality, Children, and Chauvinism," in *The Religion and Family Connection: Social Science Perspectives,* ed. Darwin L. Thomas (Provo, Utah: Bookcraft, Religious Studies Centre, Brigham Young University, 1988), 110–11.

9. Mauss, *The Angel and the Beehive,* 54, 133.

10. Tim B. Heaton and S. Calkins, "Family Size and Contraceptive Use among Mormons: 1965–75," *Review of Religious Research* 25 (1983): 103–14; and Tim B. Heaton, "The Demography of Utah Mormons," in *Utah in Demographic Perspective,* ed. T. Martin, T. Heaton, and S. Bahr (Salt Lake City: The Church of Jesus Christ of Latter-day Saints, Council of the Twelve, 1986), 112. Heaton concluded that these decisions were generally made in association with Latter-day Saints beliefs about the value of having children, involvement with LDS reference groups, and socialization in a context that favors having children.

11. Darwin L. Thomas, "Family in the Mormon Experience," in *Families and Religions: Conflict and Change in Modern Society,* ed. W. D'Antonio and J. Aldous (Beverly Hills, Calif.: Sage Publications, 1983), 267–88.

12. Jeff McClellan, "Children of Power-Assertive Parents Behave More Aggressively, Says Researcher," *Brigham Young Magazine* (February 1994): 10–12.

13. Heaton, "Four C's of the Mormon Family," 107–24.

14. W. E. Smith, "Mormon Sex Standards on College Campuses, or Deal Us Out of the Sexual Revolution," *Dialogue* 10 (February 1976): 76–81.

15. Mauss, *The Angel and the Beehive,* 151.

16. Cheryl H. Feltz, "Mormons Retrench, Stress Church's Distinctiveness," *The [Orange County, North Carolina] Herald–Sun,* Saturday, 29 January 1994, B1. Mauss, *The Angel and the Beehive.*

17. Feltz, "Mormons Retrench."
18. Address by Boyd K. Packer, October 1990, quoted in Mauss, *The Angel and the Beehive,* 206.
19. Mauss, *The Angel and the Beehive,* 51, 116, 117, 211.
20. Mauss indicates that about a third of eligible young men actually serve missions. This figure probably indicates a third of the male members of record between ages nineteen and twenty-one (Mauss, *The Angel and the Beehive,* 90).
21. "Update: Number of Converts Baptized," *Ensign* 21 (August 1991): 78.
22. "Preparing Our Youth," *Ensign* 1 (March 1971): 2.

3

Mennonite:
Family Life as
Christian Community

J. HOWARD KAUFFMAN

Mennonites are a small, conservative wing of North American Protestantism that had its beginnings in the sixteenth-century Reformation era. The twenty-some independent denominations that are currently referred to as "Mennonite" originated in 1525 in Switzerland (later in Holland) in a movement referred to by contemporary church historians as Anabaptism, the "left wing of the Reformation" or the "radical Reformation." Menno Simons, a Roman Catholic priest, converted to Anabaptism in 1536 and became the leader of the Dutch and North-German converts. Both Swiss and Dutch followers ultimately came to be called Mennonites.[1]

In 1693 a schism among the Swiss Mennonites led to the formation of the "Amish," a conservative movement led by Jacob Ammann. Seeking religious freedom, several thousand Mennonites and Amish emigrated to Pennsylvania between 1720 and 1760. Other Mennonites of Dutch origin came to the United States and Canada by way of Prussia and Russia in the late nineteenth and early twentieth centuries.

Worldwide Mennonites today number nearly 900,000 adult members, of which nearly 400,000 live in the United States and Canada.[2] This chapter limits its information to Mennonites almost entirely of European origin living in the United States and Canada. In the nineteenth century, progressive elements among the Amish formed new conferences that later identified with Mennonites.[3] The conservative remainder (approximately 60,000) are called "Old Order Amish."[4]

Much of the information provided in this chapter was obtained from surveys taken in 1972 and 1989 among Mennonite church members. The participating bodies in both surveys, together with their 1989 adult membership, included: Mennonite Church, 102,276; General Conference Mennonite Church, 62,806; Mennonite Brethren Church, 43,452; Brethren in Christ Church (affiliated with inter-Mennonite organizations such as the Mennonite World Conference and Mennonite Central

Committee), 19,853; and the Evangelical Mennonite Church, 3,888.[5]
These five groups, representing the more "progressive" of Mennonite
bodies, include the three largest Mennonite denominations.

Compared with mainline Protestant denominations, Mennonites are conservative in both theology and cultural values. However, within the Mennonite conservative-progressive continuum there are major differences. At
the conservative end are the Old Order Amish and Old Order Mennonites,
who have erected many cultural boundaries that minimize contacts with the
"outside world." At the progressive end of the continuum are the two largest
denominations, which currently are taking steps toward merger: the Mennonite Church and the General Conference Mennonite Church. The American portion of these two groups participates in some of the committees of
the National Council of the Churches of Christ in the U.S.A., although neither have formally joined the organization. The three smaller groups, with a
more evangelical orientation, have joined the National Association of Evangelicals. Sandwiched between these progressive groups and the Old Orders
are a number of small, conservative groups that have split off from the mainline Mennonite bodies within the past 125 years.

Consequently, to write about Mennonite families requires a consideration of the particular Mennonite denomination being studied. Family life among the largest Mennonite bodies compares more closely with
similar families in the large Protestant denominations than it does with
family life among the Amish. To simplify matters, the primary focus in
this chapter will be on family patterns among the more progressive Mennonites, for which more data are available, and among which communication with general American society is much more developed.

Cultural Characteristics

One hundred years ago almost all Mennonites lived on farms,
whether they were the Swiss Mennonites who settled in Pennsylvania
and states westward, or the Dutch Mennonites who settled in the prairie
states and provinces of Canada. Today one-half of Mennonites live in
cities, the other half in rural towns and villages; only 15 percent are
farmers. Despite urbanization, however, Mennonites still reflect a
strong rural bias in lifestyles and moral philosophy. Many meeting
houses are still located in the open countryside.

Nevertheless, modernization has taken place. Today, statistics show
that Mennonites in rural communities have more years of schooling and
a higher percentage of college graduates than the general rural population in the United States.

Mennonites in the cities tend to move into business and professional occupations rather than industrial and service jobs. Annual incomes are slightly higher than the national average in the United States and Canada.[6] Less than 1 percent are unemployed.

Although some 20,000 Mennonites live in Winnipeg, the largest city in Manitoba, Mennonites in the United States have tended to avoid taking up residence in the largest cities, except where mission churches are established to serve minorities (African Americans, Spanish, Chinese, Vietnamese, and so forth).[7] Only about 5 percent of North American Mennonite church members are from minority racial or ethnic groups.[8]

Mennonite family characteristics reflect a rural background with emphasis on the importance of marriage and childrearing. Table 1 indicates that only 5.5 percent of the adult population over 30 years of age have never married; a few will marry later in life. After age 45, only 2 percent of males and 5 percent of females remain single. Some 82 percent of those married at the time of the survey were still living with the original spouse. Only 4.9 percent had ever experienced divorce or separation, and more than half of these had remarried.

Table 1. Percentage Distribution of Church Members
Aged 30 and Over by Marital Status and Gender, 1989

Marital Status	Male	Female	Total
Single (never married)	4.0	6.7	5.5
Married to original spouse	88.6	76.3	82.1
Widowed	1.7	9.0	5.5
Widowed and remarried	2.0	2.0	2.0
Divorced	0.8	2.4	1.6
Divorced and remarried	2.5	3.2	2.9
Separated	0.3	0.4	0.4
Total	100.0	100.0	100.0

However, according to a 1982 census of the Mennonite Church, the 1970s marked the beginning of a downward trend in the number of children Mennonite couples were having, to the point where they equalled the national average. For two decades after World War II Mennonite birth rates were 40 to 50 percent higher than national rates. In the 1950s Mennonite families had an average of 3.7 children; by the 1970s the number had decreased to 2.3 children. By comparison, the average number of live births per Old Order Amish couple was seven.[9] The childless rate for married Mennonites is 4.4 percent, much lower, however, than the 7.5 percent national average in the United States.

Family Values as Reflected in Church Policy

From their beginnings, Mennonites have held that only the Scriptures (the New Testament in particular), rather than church tradition, are normative for doctrine and ethics. Mennonite scholars and church leaders generally do not take an "inerrantist" or "literalist" view of the Bible. As expressed in a recent official statement, the Scriptures are "the authoritative source and standard for preaching and teaching about faith and life, for distinguishing truth from error, for discerning between good and evil, and for guiding prayer and worship."[10]

Not given to formal creeds or a system of canonical law, from time to time Mennonites have adopted "confessions of faith" as a way of clarifying church policy and codifying beliefs to be used for educational purposes and as standards against which behavior could be judged.[11] The 1963 *Mennonite Confession of Faith* includes an article on marriage and the home, which states in part:

> A man shall leave his father and mother and cleave to his wife, and the two shall become one in love and mutual submission. It is God's will that marriage be a holy state, monogamous, and for life. . . . Christians shall marry only in the Lord, and for the sake of spiritual unity in the home they should become members of the same congregation. The Christian home ought regularly to have family worship, to seek faithfully to live according to the Word of God, and to support loyally the church in its mission.[12]

A new confession of faith, adopted in 1995, continues to uphold the principle of marriage as a monogamous, heterosexual, lifetime commitment: "We believe that God intends marriage to be a covenant between one man and one woman for life," and adds, "According to Scripture, right sexual union takes place only within the marriage rela- tionship."[13] This position implies that sexual intercourse is morally wrong if between unmarried persons, between a married person and someone other than the spouse, and between persons of the same sex.

Both the 1963 and the 1995 documents affirm the equal importance of persons who belong to nuclear families, to extended families, and to those who are single. Neither this assertion nor any other in the document provides a clear definition of the meaning of "family" but, by implication, unwed couples without children, and homosexual couples would not qualify as "families."

The 1963 confession makes no mention of divorce, broken marriages, or families in difficulty. The 1995 document, however, states that "The church is to minister with truth and compassion to persons in difficult family relationships. As the family of God, the church is called to be a sanctuary offering hope and healing for families." This implies that rejecting those who experience broken marriages is unacceptable, as are attitudes of rejection found in many congregations in the past and still in evidence among the more conservative bodies. Within the Old Order Amish and Old Order Mennonites, however, divorce is totally unacceptable.

One other document is important for understanding Mennonite family norms and values. After several years of study by church leaders and local congregations, a 150-page document titled "Human Sexuality in the Christian Life" was adopted in 1985 by the general assemblies of the General Conference Mennonite Church and the Mennonite Church. This report was an attempt to address the moral and ethical issues that had emerged in previous decades and to find common ground on which congregations could address specific concerns.

The document seeks to define biblical references to marriage, singleness, sexual intercourse, homosexuality, and other issues and offers them as a basis for contemporary Christian standards. The statement rejects sexual intercourse outside of marriage, including between persons of the same sex. It does, however, express the need for the churches to understand and relate kindly to persons of homosexual orientation. Although recognizing the patriarchal nature of Jewish society in biblical times, the statement affirms a Christian basis for the social equality of males and females as intimated by Galatians 3:28.

The statement did not address the issue of abortion, but it affirmed earlier statements. The 1975 and 1980 documents affirmed that abortion is unacceptable, except when the mother's life is endangered: the fetus is a form of human life and should be protected from "killing."

In a limited way, Mennonites share the prevailing Western cultural trends away from familism toward individualism. Mennonites have always stressed the importance of "community" in life and thought, in particular, the *gemeinde,* or church community—"a group of people who voluntarily join to share a common life."[14]

Mennonites are expected to live in accordance with the community's norms and values. Individuals are also responsible to a higher power, whose Holy Word specifies the standards for life and thought to which the individual is expected to conform. The idea that individuals can be the source of their own standards is unrealistic and would simply result in a normless and chaotic society.

Modern emphases on personal freedom and the concepts of self-realization and self-fulfillment tend to oppose the idea of individual responsibility to family and community. Writing from a Mennonite viewpoint, Ross Bender argues that, as a philosophy of life, individualism stands diametrically opposed to the Christian way.[15] The Christian way seeks to encourage individual growth and development within a loving and supportive environment that channels personal energies along morally constructive lines. As Robert Bellah and his associates write, "It is the moral content of relationships that allows marriages, families, and communities to persist with some certainty that there are agreed-upon standards of right and wrong that one can count on and that are not subject to incessant renegotiation."[16]

Mennonite Family Values in Practice

Although official church policy pronouncements set the standards for the life and thought of church members, not all members will reflect those standards in their daily lives. The 1972 and 1989 surveys illustrate the nature and extent of deviation from Mennonite family norms and values.

Divorce and Remarriage

Until World War II divorce among Mennonites was rare. Marriage was a lifetime commitment, a sacred vow made before God and the witness of other church members. A strict interpretation of Jesus' words in Matthew 5:31–32 excused a divorcee only if the other spouse had committed adultery. Remarriage after divorce was not accepted as long as the former spouse was living. Divorcees often experienced a certain amount of stigma, usually causing them to withdraw from the Mennonite community and join other more accepting churches.

These strict views prevailed during the 1950s and most of the 1960s, but with diminishing force, especially among the General Conference

Mennonites. By the 1970s the divorce rate had increased to the point where congregations were having to face the question of how to deal with the problem. If divorce were a sin, how could the church approve? Yet, if divorce is a sin, can it not be forgiven just as other sins can be forgiven, and hopefully forgotten? Remarriage of divorcees hinged on the question of whether this constituted adultery (as implied in Matt. 5:32), and, if so, whether it was a single act or a continuous state within the second marriage.

Of the 3,591 church members surveyed in the 1972 research, only 1 percent had ever experienced divorce or separation. By 1989, the number had risen to 4.2 percent, a significant increase. Only 1.4 percent of those members were aged 70 and older; 7.2 percent were aged 30 to 49. The number is probably underrepresented in the sample, but even if the actual percentages were double, the rate is still very low when compared with the national average.[17]

Do these numbers mean that Mennonites are more successful in marriage than the general population, or does it mean that strict views against divorce prevent unhappy couples from breaking up? The survey seems to support the former, although some of the latter may obtain.[18] Table 2 indicates that Mennonite attitudes toward divorce show a liberalizing trend. In the 1989 survey only 20 percent viewed divorce, for adultery, as "always wrong," a significant decline from the 33 percent in 1972. However, if divorce is for a cause other than adultery, a more restrictive attitude is evident. On the issue of remarriage following divorce, those checking "always wrong" dropped from 60 percent in 1972 to 31 percent in 1989.

Table 2. Mennonite Attitudes Regarding Moral Issues, 1989*

Issue	Always wrong	Sometimes wrong	Never wrong	Undecided
Divorce (for cause of adultery)	20	49	20	11
Divorce (for other causes)	35	53	2	10
Remarriage while the first spouse is still living	31	44	9	16
Premarital sexual intercourse	85	12	0.4	3
Extramarital sexual intercourse	97	2	0.3	1
Living together intimately prior to marriage	85	13	1	2
Homosexual acts	92	5	0.4	2

*Numbers indicate percentages.

Today some liberal congregations raise few questions about remarriage following divorce, provided other aspects of church relatedness are satisfactory. Some congregations follow a fairly rigorous counseling procedure before approving the remarriage of a member if the former spouse is still living. The counseling explores whether there has been sufficient healing of the broken relationships, whether obligations growing out of the former marriage are being fulfilled, whether personal factors relating to the broken marriage are understood and how these might affect the success of a subsequent marriage, and what chances there are for success in the proposed new marriage.

Sexual Standards
and Behavior

Increasing permissiveness in both attitudes and behavior in such matters as premarital sexual intercourse, cohabitation (living together unmarried), bearing children out of wedlock, unfaithfulness in marriage, abortion, pornography, and homosexual practices has been well documented. How has this "sexual revolution" affected the attitudes and behavior of Mennonites?

Mennonites historically have tended to stress the importance of holding high standards of personal morality. This stems in part from taking literally the biblical teachings against fornication and adultery, and from an emphasis on "clean living" fostered by the religious revival movements of the first half of the twentieth century. Prior to the 1950s, a couple who had premarital sexual intercourse would be expected to make a public confession of their sin. In subsequent decades private confessions would suffice.

Table 2 shows that 85 percent of the church members surveyed viewed premarital sexual intercourse as "always wrong"; another 12 percent responded "sometimes wrong." Ninety-seven percent of those surveyed regarded extramarital sexual intercourse as "always wrong." This shows that attitudes were no less restrictive in 1989. However, a liberalizing trend is evident by looking at age differences. The proportion responding "always wrong" on the issue of premarital sex varied from 77 percent for the group aged 20–29 to 94 percent for those aged 70 and over.

When queried on premarital or extramarital sex, 35 percent of those surveyed admitted to premarital intercourse; about one-half the rate of the general population.[19] Twenty-four percent of the respondents aged 50 and over admitted to premarital intercourse; 49 percent among those aged 20–49. Five percent of married respondents admitted to having sexual intercourse with someone other than the spouse. The sexual revolution has influenced some Mennonites to deviate from traditional norms, and their behavior conforms less to Mennonite norms than do their attitudes.

On the matter of living together prior to marriage, 85 percent regarded cohabitation as "always wrong," 13 percent "sometimes wrong." The 5 percent who reported having done so were in almost all cases 20 to 50 years of age.

The issue of homosexuality is causing considerable stress among Mennonites. Strong views regarding homosexual practice as sin are expressed in the letters to the editor of church papers. The stigma involved in being recognized as homosexual is such that most homosexuals do not reveal their sexual orientation, despite official policy that urges acceptance of homosexuals if they are nonpracticing. Only a few congregations accept known practicing homosexuals as members, a situation that has precipitated requests to district conferences that such congregations be removed from conference membership. Ninety-two percent of the respondents to the 1989 survey regarded homosexual acts as "always wrong" (see Table 2). Some 32 percent would deny membership in a congregation to a person of known homosexual orientation, even if not practicing; another 48 percent would permit membership, but deny leadership positions; and only 12 percent would accept ordination to the ministry if the person were otherwise qualified. However, if a homosexual is currently engaged in homosexual acts, only 22 percent would permit membership in a congregation; only 2 percent would allow ordination.

Table 3 indicates Mennonite attitudes toward abortion in the 1972 and 1989 surveys. The respondents were asked whether they thought it "should be possible for a pregnant woman to obtain a *legal* abortion," that is, whether the national laws should permit abortions under varying circumstances. Note that the question is not whether an abortion is morally right, but whether that choice should be permitted by law.

Table 3. Percentage of Church Members Approving Legal Abortion under Varying Circumstances, 1972 and 1989

Circumstance	1972	1989
If the woman's health is seriously endangered	73	53
If pregnant as a result of rape	46	31
If strong chance of serious defect in the baby	49	23
If the family cannot afford more children	12	4
If not married and does not want to marry the man	9	4
If she does not want the baby	8	5

It is only in the case of a threat to the mother's life that a majority of Mennonites would approve legal abortion. Each question shows an increasingly conservative outlook between those polled in 1972 and those polled in 1989. However, in both surveys some 10 to 30 percent of the respondents, depending on the circumstance, checked the "uncertain" response, indicating that many were unable to arrive at a clear opinion. It was surprising to discover that attitudes toward abortion had hardened in the seventeen-year interim, perhaps influenced by the increasingly vocal pro-life movement following the *Roe v. Wade* Supreme Court decision in 1973. It is not surprising, then, to see that in the 1989 survey only 2.3 percent of the females indicated they had had a planned abortion.

Family Structures

Contemporary Mennonite family authority structures can be seen as a product of two historical streams of development: biblical and cultural. Mennonites have leaned heavily on the Bible for guidance in doctrine and ethics, but social experience has also played an influential role in developing cultural norms and values, modifying a cut-and-dried biblical literalism.

Within the family, the balance of power and authority is usually weighted toward the male side of the family, although the contemporary movement toward gender equality in North American society has balanced the sides somewhat. Currently, policy statements and the tone of church literature favor norms of equality between spouses. Data from surveys in 1956 and 1989 show a gradual shift toward more equal sharing of authority and more overlap of gender roles between Mennonite husbands and wives.[20]

Table 4 reveals that a strong third (36 percent) of married respondents view their power sharing as equal, although 55 percent of wives regarded the husband as leader—28 percent "definitely," and 27 percent "slightly." Only 8 percent of males and females perceived the wife as leader, most only "slightly."

A significant element in these findings is that marriages do not conform to one specific type but are determined by individual personalities and relationships.

Demographics indicate clearly the modernization among Mennonites. Female employment is a good example. At the beginning of the twentieth century few women were employed outside the home. The 1990s show that employment among Mennonite women, including

Table 4. Power-Sharing between Mennonite Spouses, by Gender, 1989*

Responses	Males (N = 1205)	Females (N = 1252)	Total (N = 2457)
Husband definitely	19	28	24
Husband slightly	37	27	32
Equal	37	36	36
Wife slightly	6	7	6
Wife definitely	1	2	2
Total	100	100	100

*Respondents were asked: Who is dominant (takes the lead) in the marriage relationship?
N represents the total number of respondents surveyed.
Numbers indicate percentage of those surveyed.

married women, equals the national average. One reason for this is that most Mennonites live in the industrialized areas of the United States and Canada, where employment is fairly easily obtained.

In 1972 the majority of employed women worked outside the home only part time; in 1989 the majority were employed full time. In 1989, among married women with one or more preschool children, 47 percent were employed, compared to the national average of 56 percent.[21]

This may partially account for the fact that 62 percent of the respondents agreed that "household tasks should be shared nearly equally between husband and wife," although there was considerable support for role differentiation.

There was much ambivalence regarding the matter of career development for married women. While nearly two-thirds agreed that "the woman's career development should be given as high a priority as the man's," more than half felt that "women today are neglecting their family responsibilities by going outside the home to work on a full-time, career basis."

Households with Children

Nearly all Mennonite children are reared in stable two-parent homes. According to the 1989 survey, 57 percent of the households contained one or more children. Among these households with children, 91.2 percent were headed by a married couple in their first marriage, 5.3 percent were stepfamilies; only 2.3 percent were headed by a single parent; 1.2 percent were headed by widows. There were no unmarried, single-parent families among those surveyed.

Only a small proportion of Mennonite children experience the emotional trauma of the divorce of their parents. Approximately 5 percent of households with children were headed by a parent who was divorced (not remarried) or divorced and remarried.

Undergirding Marriage and Family Life

What programs have been generated in the decades since World War II to counter the threats to Mennonite family life and to encourage desirable changes? Focus on the family by denominational agencies was rather weak in the first two decades after the war. Limited budgets forced Mennonite denominations to devote little time to family life education, and it was not until the 1970s that a part-time secretarial position was created in this area.

The secretary encouraged and assisted district conferences to establish family-serving programs, promoted workshops on marriage and family enrichment (frequently modeled after the Marriage Encounter program developed in Catholic parishes), and promoted the production of literature on Christian family life. Mennonite representation on the Church and Family Committee of the National Council of Churches provided a pipeline for program ideas generated by Protestant denominations.

Sunday schools have stressed the importance of home Bible study and family worship, promoting the idea that "the family that prays together stays together." Seventy percent of Mennonite church members offer prayer before all meals; another 20 percent "at most meals." About one-third of the households (down from 45 percent in 1972) have a family worship period at least several times a week in addition to prayers at meals. Publications such as *Rejoice* and *Christian Living* support family and individual worship, publishing articles on marriage, parenting, and child development.

The Mennonite Board of Congregational Ministries designated 1974 as a year of special emphasis on the Christian family, highlighted by a "Week of Work" in Chicago where approximately seventy clergy and laypersons reviewed the nature and problems of marriage and family living. The workshop identified the needs for (1) a biblical understanding of Christian family living, (2) development of a Christian support system, (3) personal growth, (4) role identification, and (5) the improvement of marriage relationships. In 1973, 1987, and 1992 there were conferences on aging that included a focus on the home life and problems of aging couples and widows.

Church-related educational institutions also play a role in strengthening Mennonite family life, although a majority of Mennonite children and youth attend public schools and universities.

Summary and Conclusions

Mennonites are a conservative religious group struggling to preserve traditional family values in a world filled with family casualties and weakening family values and family support systems. Mennonites tend to resist growing public attitudes that regard single-parent families, cohabitation outside of marriage, and homosexual companionship as of equal value to intact two-parent families. The family-affirming cultural values of the 1950s still prevail in Mennonite circles, but with increased understanding and acceptance of the more important role of women within and beyond the family.

Mennonites continue to believe the following things about marriage and family.

1. Marriage is a spiritual vow to permanence until the death of one of the spouses, therefore divorce is wrong, but forgivable.
2. To be single is of no less value than to be married.
3. Sexual intercourse outside the bonds of legal marriage is wrong.
4. Children are a blessing to parents and kinsfolk (how many is optional).
5. Children should have the privilege of being reared by two parents (fatherless homes are viewed as deficient).
6. Human life, including fetal life, is sacred and should not be violated.
7. Resources must be provided to help prevent marriage and family breakdown, as well as to assist and support individuals when breakdown occurs.
8. Kinsfolk are expected to come to the assistance of members experiencing social, emotional, or economic difficulties.

Among Mennonites, maintaining these intrinsic values is not to be seen as an individual enterprise. Individualism is a danger—too tempting to persons to chart their own moral paths; too risky, for wrong paths can be chosen out of lack of experience or lack of control over emotions. Mennonites believe that standards must be derived from the *gemeinde*, the church, the congregation of like-minded believers, and they must result from long and careful consideration by those who share life together. But even the church is not the final source of moral standards, because behind all human deliberations is the Holy Word—the word and will of God, insofar as it can be understood. Mennonites see the solution to contemporary family problems as a greater acceptance of the Holy Word as a guide to life and through active work by churches in determining moral standards and in proclaiming them more courageously and forthrightly.

NOTES

1. Cornelius J. Dyck, *An Introduction to Mennonite History,* 3d ed. (Scottdale, Pa.: Herald Press, 1993).
2. Diether G. Lichdi, *Mennonite World Handbook* (Carol Stream, Ill.: Mennonite World Conference, 1990), 321–27.
3. Theron F. Schlabach, *Peace, Faith, Nation: Mennonites and Amish in Nineteenth-Century America* (Scottdale, Pa.: Herald Press, 1988), chap. 8.
4. Although occasional references to the Old Order Amish will be made in this chapter, space requirements limit our treatment to the Mennonites.
5. In the 1972 survey a stratified-random sample of 3,591 church members from 174 congregations in the United States and Canada completed a lengthy questionnaire. The findings were published in J. Howard Kauffman and Leland Harder, *Anabaptists Four Centuries Later* (Scottdale, Pa.: Herald Press, 1975). A similar survey in 1989 of 3,083 respondents was published in J. Howard Kauffman and Leo Driedger, *The Mennonite Mosaic* (Scottdale, Pa.: Herald Press, 1991). The 231,305 members of the five participating denominations constituted 77 percent of the total membership of the eighteen independent denominations identified as Mennonites. The nonparticipating bodies are mostly small, conservative, splinter groups. Of the total Mennonite and Amish membership, 73 percent live in the United States and 27 percent in Canada.
6. Kauffman and Driedger, *The Mennonite Mosaic,* 114.
7. Leo Driedger, *Mennonites in Winnipeg* (Winnipeg: Kindred Press, 1990).
8. Michael L. Yoder, "Findings from the 1982 Mennonite Census," *The Mennonite Quarterly Review* 59 (October 1985): 313.
9. John A. Hostetler, *Amish Society,* 4th ed. (Baltimore: Johns Hopkins University Press, 1993).
10. *Confession of Faith in a Mennonite Perspective* (Scottdale, Pa.: Herald Press, 1995), 21.

11. Among Mennonite bodies we can speak of "church policy" only in a general sense. Mennonite polity is congregational and there are no denominational laws, controls, or canonical courts as in the Roman Catholic or Anglican confessions. District conferences exercise a certain amount of control over congregations, but mainly in the approval of ordinations. Denominational doctrine and ethics derive from "confessions of faith" and conference resolutions that establish standards of belief and practice that become grounds for judging the behavior of church members. Church discipline tends to be informal, and only the most flagrant violations would be sanctioned at the district or denominational level. Hence, in the strictest sense, there is no "family policy" among Mennonites, only standards of belief and practice that, nevertheless, have considerable effect in guiding the behavior of individuals and groups. Individuals who deviate from these standards risk becoming "out of fellowship" within their congregations.

12. *Mennonite Confession of Faith* (Scottdale, Pa.: Herald Press, 1963), 21.

13. *Confession of Faith in a Mennonite Perspective,* 72.

14. Calvin Redekop, *Mennonite Society* (Baltimore: The Johns Hopkins University Press, 1989), 62.

15. Ross T. Bender, *Christians in Families* (Scottdale, Pa.: Herald Press, 1982), 42.

16. Robert N. Bellah et al., *Habits of the Heart: Individualism and Commitment in American Life* (New York: Harper & Row, 1985), 139.

17. Andrew J. Cherlin, *Marriage, Divorce, Remarriage,* revised and enlarged (Cambridge: Harvard University Press, 1992). Cherlin estimates that at current rates, about half of all marriages in the United States will end in divorce.

18. J. Howard Kauffman, "Interpersonal Relations in Traditional and Emergent Family Types Among Midwest Mennonites," *Marriage and Family Living* 23 (August 1961): 247–52.

19. David A. Schulz, in *The Changing Family* (Englewood Cliffs, N.J.: Prentice-Hall, 1982), summarized some twenty American studies and concluded that upward of 50 percent of females and 75 percent of males experienced premarital intercourse in the 1970s, and that number has increased since then.

20. For statistical data and analysis see Chapter 5 in Kauffman and Driedger, *The Mennonite Mosaic;* also J. Howard Kauffman, "Power and Authority in Mennonite Families," *The Mennonite Quarterly Review* 68 (October 1994): 500–523.

21. Otto Johnson, ed., *Information Please Almanac* (Boston: Houghton Mifflin, 1990).

4

Catholic:
Family Unity and Diversity
within the Body of Christ

CHRISTINE FIRER HINZE

The Catholic community's experience on two sides of a historical watershed forms the organizing focus of this sketch of Roman Catholic families in the United States between 1945 and 1990. The 1960s, a time of social upheaval for most Americans, constituted an even greater turning point for Catholics in America.

> The Catholic community, perhaps more than any other religious community in the U.S., experienced the combined and simultaneously stimulating and disintegrating hurricane winds of social and religious reform and upheaval that blew across the country in the 1960s and early 1970s. The implementation of the second Vatican council's [1962–65] liturgy and structural reforms and the corresponding transformation of American Catholic consciousness that accompanied them took place at a time of revolutionary change in American political and cultural life.[1]

Between 1965 and 1990, "reforms, rebellions, school and parish closings, and a dramatic decline in denominational identification shook and transformed a community whose most recent experience and memory was one of relative institutional stability, unity, and phenomenal growth."[2]

As they navigated the treacherous waters of these years, U.S. Catholics maintained a worldview accompanied by characteristic values, attitudes, and practices.[3] Never monolithically expressed, this worldview harbored tensions that were refracted differently before and after the mid-1960s. Throughout, however, at least three "family resemblances" can be discerned.

A first common thread is diversity and responses to it. Internal heterogeneity, along with certain differences between Catholics and their non-Catholic fellow citizens, persisted. Second, Catholic religiosity comprises distinctive ecclesial and doctrinal structures, piety and moral practices, and approaches to social action. This religiosity is suffused with an in-the-bones appreciation of creation, sacramentality, and incarnation on the one hand, and a focus on law and institutional organization on the other. A third characteristic of the Catholic community in the United States is its tensive relationship to American institutions and culture. The period culminated a long quest by Catholics to gain acceptance as American citizens. But a strong strand of Catholic counterculturalism also decried secularism, individualism, and materialism. As Catholic families negotiated the crossing between the 1940s and the 1990s, expressions of each of these common features continued to evolve.

Families in a Church
"Coming of Age": 1945–1965

Between 1945 and 1965, the U.S. Catholic population increased by a stunning 90 percent to 45.6 million. Enrollments in Catholic elementary and secondary schools soared more than 120 percent and in Catholic colleges and universities by 300 percent. The 1960 election of John F. Kennedy as the first Roman Catholic president symbolized, for many, the full acceptance of American Catholics into the public mainstream.[4] Change meant growth during those years, and a burgeoning Euro-American Catholic middle class pursued being American and being Catholic with equal vigor.

Diversity

By the late 1940s, Catholics, historically regarded as "different" by the majority Protestant culture, felt more enfranchised as Americans, and Catholic families bore their differences more comfortably than ever before.[5] The urban parish neighborhoods so many Euro-American Catholics called home had even received Hollywood's sentimental accolade in the 1944 film *Going My Way,* featuring Bing Crosby's Oscar-winning performance as Father O'Malley. Younger Catholic families were beginning to gravitate toward upscale neighborhoods at the city's edges or in the suburbs, away from the distinctly bounded Catholic enclaves of their parents. But they still stood out when they sent their uniformed children to parochial schools, engaged in mysterious devotional practices, abstained from meat on Fridays, or declined invitations to weddings of their Protestant neighbors. As a group too, Catholics registered lower divorce rates, slightly higher family sizes, and more conservative attitudes toward birth control, premarital sex, and abortion than other citizens.

The challenges of internal diversity continued and increased. By the 1940s, U.S. Catholic pastors had been adjudicating distinctions and conflicts among different Catholic "nationalities" for over a century.[6] European ethnic diversity still dominated the attention of an overwhelmingly Euro-American Catholic leadership. Intermarriage between Catholics of different ethnicities could still cause family divisions. Religiously "mixed marriages" elicited profound dismay.[7] Among the growing Catholic middle class, however, ethnic intermarriage increased, blurring longstanding communal distinctions.

Growing numbers of Hispanic-American and African-American Catholic families migrated to the cities, where they were alternately disregarded, marginalized, or spurned by their Euro-American counterparts.[8] Black or Hispanic parishes and missions reflected earlier patterns of ethnic separation, but segregation was also frequently maintained for racist reasons.[9] The traditional Catholic family and parish were pictured as Euro-American, not African- or Hispanic-American. A black or Hispanic Father O'Malley would have been unthinkable.

Socio-economic diversity also persisted. Numbers of Catholic college graduates increased, and more Euro-American Catholics attained white-collar job status. But their traditional support for labor continued, as did allegiance to the Democratic party. Hispanic and black Catholic families remained far more likely to be among the poor or working poor.

Religiosity

Church Structure and Parish Life

For millions of Catholic families during the 1940s and 1950s, life revolved around Catholicity, parish, and neighborhood. Especially in the large northern cities,[10] the world of postwar Catholic piety was symbolized by the imposing presence of a large parish plant with a staff of religious sisters and priests, in a neighborhood created by parish boundaries. Among urban Catholics, "who you were and where you were from" was framed in terms of parish—"I'm from Resurrection," "She married a boy from Lady of Sorrows," and so forth. These years consolidated a transition from an older model of the parish as an immigrant fortress reflecting ethnic loyalty, to the parish as a religious enclave evoking denominational pride and allegiance.[11]

Catholic family religiosity was strongly influenced by church teaching and structure, piety, and Catholic action that stressed on the one side the family's spiritual role as cell in the great "Mystical Body of Christ," working to supernaturally elevate the world,[12] and on the other side the family's institutional role as a "praying, paying, and obeying" Catholic household within the local parish and, ultimately, within the Roman Catholic church. Religiosity was a pervasive affair that for Euro-American Catholic families revolved around parish and parochial school participation. Hispanic and black Catholic families' religiosity, on the other hand, often selectively incorporated church into the extended family experience.

Theology and Teachings on Marriage and the Family

Official teachings and theology rooted the Catholic family in the heterosexual, monogamous, lifelong, procreative bond of Christian marriage. Catholic theologians defined children as marriage's primary purpose.[13] Christian families' tasks were imbued with a supernatural aim: to bear "children who are to become members of the church of Christ, to raise up 'citizens with the saints and also members of the household of God' (Eph. 2:19), that the worshippers of God and our Savior may daily increase."[14] Parents intimately collaborated with God's creative and redemptive activity, mediated through the sacraments and discipline of the Catholic Church.

Official documents and confessors' manuals disclose a church whose jurisdiction extended to the intimate details of a couple's spiritual and sexual life.[15] Men's and women's familial roles were clearly differentiated. Fatherhood was most often mentioned in terms of a man's right to fulfill his role as head of the family by supporting it financially. The traditional assumption, based on Ephesians 5, that man is "chief of the family, and head of the wife" endured, but Popes Pius XI (1922–39) and XII (1939–58) emphasized an "order of love" in the family that encompassed the genuine equality of men and women in human dignity and supernatural destiny.[16] For women, this order precluded "exaggerated liberty which cares not for the good of the family; it forbids that in this body which is the family, the heart be separated from the head. . . . For if the man is the head, the woman is the heart, and as he occupies the chief place in ruling, so she may and ought to claim for herself the chief place in love."[17]

As married women's participation in the paid labor force increased during the postwar years, Pope Pius XII again warned against false understandings of equality that might lead a woman to abandon "the home where she [has] reigned as queen, and [to] her subjection to the same work strain and working hours [as men]."[18] Such false equality depreciates "her true dignity and the solid foundation of all her rights which is her characteristic feminine role, and the intimate coordination of the two sexes." Both conservative and progressive U.S. Catholic families of the period supported these views concerning gender.[19] Prohibitions against remarriage following divorce, artificial birth control, abortion, homosexual relations, and extramarital sexual activity were also widely accepted. Nonconformists were regarded—and regarded themselves— as having fallen short of being "good Catholics."

Family Piety and Moral Practice

Much pre-Vatican II American Catholic piety relied on family socialization and participation. Families attended Mass on Sundays and Holy Days, ensured that their children received the sacraments, followed fasting rules, and participated in family devotions such as the home rosary. Catholics' taste for material mediation assured the popularity of all kinds of so-called external sacramentals. Medals, rosary beads, holy cards bearing images of saints or prayers promising the supplicant indulgences against time to be spent in purgatory, missals, statues, votive candles, and crucifixes were common accoutrements in Catholic homes. Many families also owned an approved Catholic translation of the Bible, but it was more likely to be picked up to record births, marriages, and deaths on the "Family Record" pages than for devotional reading.

Threading through this communal religiosity was a deep spiritual individualism focused on the saving of one's own soul. Ecclesial rituals such as "hearing" the Latin Mass, silent "holy hours" of prayer before the exposed Blessed Sacrament (the consecrated bread worshiped as the Body of the Savior), and frequent private confession of sins to a priest, underscored this conversation between the individual soul and God. Helping bridge the chasm between oneself and the Almighty were a panoply of angels and saints, and Mary under many titles. Among black Catholics, piety surrounding Jesus often served an analogous function.

Variegated and richly affective family spiritualities flourished amid (sometimes in genial contrast to) the clearly defined, heavily cognitive context of Catholic Church doctrine and discipline. The Baltimore Catechism distilled the faith to a series of questions and answers that could be memorized. A sacralized, hierarchical authority structure extended from one's local parish priests, through the bishops, to the pope, and through him, to God. Regulations concerning all aspects of faith and life, continually refined by canon lawyers and moral theologians, provided Catholic families' popular devotion and practices with a trusted institutional scaffolding.

Mary Reed Newland's widely read 1954 manual, *We and Our Children: Molding the Child in Christian Living,* offers a glimpse of the duties urged upon Euro-American Catholic parents, especially mothers, in the 1950s.[20] The author offers mothers advice on nurturing holiness in children, especially by helping youngsters cultivate virtue and ward off vice. Sex education, for instance, is treated in a chapter titled "Purity." Besides reflecting a 1950s American Catholic attitude toward sexual virtue, Newland's sympathetic but firm treatment of the problem of "self-stimulation" among young children illustrates how sexual teaching, Marian piety, and images of good mothering were intertwined.[21] The mother who encouraged purity, did not express anger with lack of success, but patiently assisted the child in such "struggles with concupiscence," reflected a strong, comforting and forgiving image of the divine that many Catholics found mediated by Mary. The struggle for virtue and the path to heaven was arduous but to be renewed daily with the promise of God's forgiveness and grace, reliably administered through the church. Mutually reinforcing home and church influences sought to equip young Catholics for the fight, furnishing children's imaginations with luminous images of saints, angels, and the devil, and of heaven, hell, and purgatory.

Among Hispanic-American Catholics, practices surrounding sacraments, Mary, and the saints were more firmly situated in extended-family settings.[22] Religious socialization of Mexican children took place largely in the home, in a tradition called "religion *casera.*"[23] Wedding customs illustrated how popular piety encompassed regulated Roman rituals. Pre- and postnuptial neighborhood processions and family-based ceremonies combined sacramentals, such as rosaries, with personal blessings given by parents, *padrinos* (godparents and sponsors), and other significant family members.[24] *Santa Maria* (Mary) held pride of place in Mexican-American family piety, particularly under her title as Our Lady of Guadalupe.[25] For every major feast or religious rite of passage, "Hispanic Catholics in North America employed a little tradition that linked their religion to their family-centered culture. Faced with the imposition of a great tradition by an ecclesiastical institution that was unwilling to be mutually influenced, many surrendered the institutional Church in order to preserve an expressive one."[26]

African-American Catholics frequently participated in all-black parishes whose structures, rituals, and associations closely resembled those in Euro-American parishes. The life that black Catholic families breathed into these externals, however, bore the stamp of their unique history as a caste-like minority within a hostile dominant culture, and testified to the strength and resiliency of African-American families.[27] Black families' religiosity reflected a Christocentric piety,[28] a sense of church as extended family, and strong participation in parish-related associations reflecting the history of lay initiative and accountability within black churches. Spirituality was expressed in vibrant communal worship, prayer and devotions in the home, and in public pageantry.[29] African-American Catholic religiosity reinforced the functions that the black family played in empowering members to endure and resist discrimination. Conversely, the extended-family-help system, whose elastic boundaries often included friends and church members who were like family or "fictive kin," stood at the crux of the faith life of black Catholics.

Families, "Catholic Action," and Society

Episcopal pronouncements during the cold war years exhorted laypersons to permeate civilization with the Christian spirit and to combat communism and secularism at home and abroad. Bishops declared secularism as "the practical exclusion of God from human thinking and living" that, besides threatening the social order, attacked the family at its roots by fomenting divorce, birth control, and economic injustice.[30] Responding to the call to Christianize the social order, many families joined associations dedicated to family spirituality or Catholic social action.[31] The two most popular, the Cana Conference and the Christian Family Movement, arose in the 1940s. Both were lay-led family apostolates extending beyond the direct control of parish clergy.[32] Both reflected an ongoing dialectic between associations focused on Catholic couples' and families' internal life—the thrust of Cana's marriage renewal agenda, and those emphasizing public engagement—as in CFM's mission to "reform those conditions in society [wreaking] havoc on the integrity of modern family life."[33] These lay movements were more family-focused and less radical than communities such as Dorothy Day's Catholic Worker movement, or Canadian Catherine de Hueck's Friendship Houses. But more countercultural forms of Catholic action indirectly influenced family apostolates through venues such as *Integrity* magazine (1946–56), which "articulated a radical personalist critique of American individualism and capitalism and fostered a sacramental-personalist approach to family living."[34]

Black Catholic pious and charitable associations, especially the Knights and Ladies of St. Peter Claver, drew ever-larger memberships during this period. The Knights and Ladies, besides being the main social organizations in many black parishes, became nationally chartered. These groups also transcended earlier, conservative positions on race, to lend support to civil rights alliances such as the NAACP and the Urban League.[35]

A Renewing and Pluralist Church: 1965–1990

In 1962, Pope John XXIII convened the Second Vatican Council, charging the world's bishops with a pastoral task: to discern and proclaim, in light of the "signs of the times," the ancient Catholic faith in a manner appropriate to the modern world. "Renewal," implying a return to the deep wellsprings of the faith, and *Aggiornamento* or "updating," were the words most often used to describe the Council's intended impact.

Vatican deliberations had direct repercussions on American Catholic families. Most visible and symbolic were changes in public worship, especially the replacement of Latin by English in the Mass and the reconfiguration of eucharistic worship in horizontal-communal idiom, rather than the transcendent and privatized format that had predominated. Also of great consequence was the renewal and modernization of the clergy and religious orders, leading nuns and priests to resign in great numbers between 1965 and 1975.[36]

The transformation of the 1950s parish resulted in staffing deficits contributing to a third significant effect of Vatican II—the ascendance of laypersons in institutional church ministry and leadership. Conciliar pronouncements inspired a sea-change in American Catholics' orienting ecclesial imagery. The older model of an organically connected, but deeply hierarchical institution gave way to a communal model of church as "the People of God." Though still excluded from priesthood, appropriately credentialed lay women and married men began to fill the breach left by departing sisters and priests. By 1990, parish schools and religious education programs were staffed nearly wholly by laity. Many other aspects of parish pastoral life formerly controlled by priests became the responsibility of qualified lay ministers. Families were far more likely to encounter parish ministers who were also laypersons, with families of their own.

Controversy erupted following the issuance of Pope Paul VI's 1968 encyclical *Humanae Vitae,* which reiterated the traditional prohibition of artificial birth control. This reaction exemplified a dramatic shift in opinion and practice that was occurring among Catholic families. By the late 1980s, polls revealed that over 90 percent of lay Catholics rejected the birth control ban, regarding birth control as a matter for individual couples to decide. For the first time in memory, large numbers of the faithful disavowed certain aspects of church teaching, yet remained confident and hopeful about their status as "good Catholics." The significance of this development cut more deeply than the presenting controversy itself because it heralded a fundamental shift in the relationship between many Catholic families and the teaching authority of the church.

Religious upheaval was paralleled by demographic changes. By 1990, many families had moved to the suburbs, although three out of four Catholics still lived in or near cities. Between 1965 and 1988, enrollments in Catholic primary and secondary schools declined, yet those of Catholic colleges and universities increased by 46 percent, and the percentage of Catholics with a college education more than doubled. Church membership increased, but the numbers of tenuously affiliated or unchurched Catholic families also grew. By 1991, 58 million U.S. citizens—24.1 percent of the population—were active Roman Catholics. Another 15 million identified themselves as Catholic, but not as active participants.[37]

Diversity

The Catholic ethnic and racial landscape continued to evolve after 1965.[38] Civil rights movements of the 1960s galvanized non-European American Catholics, leading many to fight for greater enfranchisement within their church. Recognition of culturally diverse familial practices grew, along with diversity of familial forms and separate identities among certain communities.

As Catholic family demographics followed societal trends, parishes began to address the presence of single parents and blended families in their midst. Ministries of support for divorced persons and their children, chapters of Parents Without Partners, even organizations supporting homosexual Catholics and their families, sprang up. Church leaders cautiously insisted that such groups work within the bounds of traditional church teachings. On another front, the number of Catholic women entering the paid work force during these years is one indication that women's rights and economic need had the same impact on Catholic women as on women of other denominations.[39]

By the mid-1980s, national opinion research showed that in general, U.S. Catholic attitudes and practices with respect to nontraditional family forms resembled those of the general population, with some exceptions. Predictably, more widespread disapproval of abortion, and a slightly lower divorce rate persisted. But Catholics also expressed significantly greater tolerance for nontraditional sexual practices, for a range of family forms, for ethnic and racial diversity in neighborhoods, as well as stronger support for women's rights than members of other Christian groups.[40]

During the decades following the Vatican Council, black and Hispanic Catholic clergy and laity began to be included in official church leadership. Both communities held national gatherings—*Encuentros* and black Catholic Congresses—where representatives met to discover ways to minister more effectively to their peoples and families. By the 1980s, Catholic families in these communities were lending their voices to the deliberations out of which official pronouncements and pastoral plans developed.[41]

A more troubling form of diversity—more precisely, division—also intensified between 1965 and 1990. In the mid-1980s, 74 percent of Catholics still lived in urban areas, roughly divided evenly between center city and suburbs.[42] But the socio-economic and racial complexions of city and suburban Catholic populations became increasingly dichotomous. Official pronouncements and practical inroads toward solidarity with the poor and against racism notwithstanding, de facto segregation of many parishes along racial and socio-economic lines persisted and at times even increased. Some perceived, with alarm, the emergence of a two-tiered church: "One level is white, middle-class, and suburban; the other is brown and black, lower-class, and urban. Neither one talks very much to the other and the lower-class church feels especially alienated from the rest of the American Catholic Church."[43]

Religiosity

Church Structure and Parish Life

The parish's role in Euro-American Catholic families' lives declined after the 1960s, due in part to the isolation of the suburbs. Although urban parishes remained, and some thrived, losses of more affluent members to the suburbs, plus "white flight" from large northern cities, took their toll. As older churches lovingly constructed by European immigrants deteriorated in the central cities, a new wave of church-building occurred in suburbia. But the commitment to parochial schools that had fired previous generations of Euro-American Catholics dampened where reputable public school systems existed. Some parishes redirected resources into adult- or family-centered religious education. In the cities too, parish schools closed, often due to insufficient funds and against the desires of parish and neighborhood families. By the 1980s, the decline of parish schools appeared to be reversing, but the importance of an overriding parish commitment to maintaining a parochial school continued to be debated.[44]

Theology and Teachings on Marriage and the Family

In this time of flux, teachings on marriage and family were subjected to scholarly and popular rethinking. Official statements continued to reiterate traditional doctrines, yet subtle developments occurred in the theological presentation of marriage, in the constitution of family, and in the roles of men and women in church and society.

Beginning with Vatican II and *Humanae Vitae,* official teachings, while reaffirming procreativity as a constitutive dimension of Christian marriage, set aside the language of hierarchy of ends that had described procreation as marriage's "primary" purpose. This unobtrusive move opened the door for a more multidimensional and personalist understanding of marital sexuality that highlighted its loving and bonding, as well as its procreative purposes.[45]

The 1980s saw an upsurge of official attention to the family as a focal point for theological and pastoral concern. Pope John Paul's 1981 *Familiaris Consortio* identified four functions of families: to form "an intimate community of persons"; to serve the physical and spiritual transmission of life; to participate in developing society "by becoming a community of social training and hospitality, as well as a community of political involvement and activity"; and to share in the life and mission of the church by becoming a believing, evangelizing, and praying community that also serves the neighbor.[46] Inspired by the pope, and also by concern for families in an individualist decade, the U.S. bishops declared the 1980s a "decade of the family," and mounted a campaign to promote a "family perspective in church and society" in every diocese and parish.[47]

The bishops defined "family" in carefully chosen words that both affirmed tradition and signaled a new recognition of pluralism: "The family is an intimate community of persons bound together by blood, marriage, or adoption for the whole of life. In our Catholic tradition, the family proceeds from marriage—an intimate, exclusive, permanent, and faithful partnership of husband and wife." Supporting literature explained that this definition was meant to include living kin, ancestors, and descendants; to recognize that many persons are involved simultaneously in several families; to include single persons (significant in light of the skyrocketing numbers of persons residing alone); to acknowledge other convenantal relationships in families besides marriage, for example, between parents and children, siblings, and others that can outlive a marriage itself; and to honor the special relationships established by adoption.[48]

Scholarly interest in theologies of the family began to supplant earlier preoccupations with marriage and sexuality. References at Vatican II to family as "domestic church," amplified by Pope John Paul II, prompted study of early Christian understandings of the family as the church of the home.[49] Official declarations that "the family is not merely like the Church, but is truly Church," impelled new theological reflection on the family as an *ecclesiola* with a unique mission of internal communion and public witness.[50]

The Catholic "family perspective" articulated in these pastoral documents recognizes each family as "a living and developing system whose members are essentially interconnected." It respects family diversity. This perspective, finally, is committed to the proposition that "partnerships need to be formed between families and institutions that share family responsibilities."[51] As the new decade of the 1990s dawned, this Catholic theological vision of family continued to germinate. Meanwhile, many Catholic families went about their daily lives unaware either of the family decade that had just transpired or of the lofty and provocative mission that their leadership had begun to propose for them.

Official teaching concerning men's and women's family roles also underwent subtle change. Popes John XXIII and Paul VI affirmed the equal status and rights of women and men in society.[52] John Paul II gives "the dignity and proper role of woman" extended treatment, but reasserts an explicit theology of male-female complementarity. In order to uphold families, society must protect women's special vocation in the home. "True advancement of women" requires that they should "not have to pay for their advancement by abandoning what is specific to them and at the expense of the family, in which women as mothers have an irreplaceable role."[53] Although the importance of fathers in families is noted, the pontiff's words reverberate with echoes of a breadwinner/ homemaker gender division. Men, it is implied, are indispensable as breadwinners, and appreciated in—but not fundamentally meant for— the domestic role. For women, the reverse is suggested.[54] Some U.S. Catholics embraced these papal insights, but others perceived signs of a "dual anthropology" that separated male and female natures to the detriment of both families and society.[55]

Family Piety and Moral Practice

Catholic families' spirituality and morality were reoriented by the changes of the 1960s. Structured, individually focused devotions such as the rosary gave way somewhat to free-form, interpersonal practices like spontaneous group prayers before meals or bedtime, or "prayer groups" rather than Altar and Rosary Guilds. Devotional Bible reading increased, but still lagged behind that of Protestants. A greater emphasis on personal conscience may explain declines in such "required" practices as Sunday Mass attendance.[56] But Catholic families continued to seek out the sacraments, and some practices, such as personal prayer and reception of communion, increased.

What of the religio-moral imaginations of Catholic families during those tumultuous years? Some research suggests that, despite changing patterns of observance, a lively interior religious life persisted among younger and older Catholic families. But Catholic piety featured a significant shift away from legalistic, commanding, and judging images of the Divine, to more gracious, friend- or lover-like, and forgiving imagery.[57] This finding, if reliable, may illuminate two other changes reported among post-Vatican II Catholics: "a shift from an appeal to institutional church leadership to God, and a conviction that God does not want you to stay away from church because you reject a specific teaching of the church."[58]

Families, "Catholic Action," and Society

By the late 1960s, the Christian Family Movement had waned, foundering on internal conflicts concerning its focus on family renewal or social action. Declining denominationalism during the 1970s and 1980s redirected some lay Catholic activism into ecumenical or secular efforts, such as the Nuclear Freeze and ecological movements. The

1980s also witnessed a stream of church teachings on economic, political, and cultural matters, some highly publicized. Many families imbibed the message that Catholicism entailed action for justice, and some sought solidarity in new groups such as the St. Louis-based Parenting for Peace and Justice Network.[59] The pro-life emphasis of official teachings inspired some Catholics to join movements dedicated to natural family planning, or the protection of pre-born children. Other intentional associations dedicated to spiritually based social action, like Maryknoll lay missioners or the Jesuit-affiliated Christian Life Communities, sought to embrace whole families in the dual mission of nurturing religious community, and instigating social justice.

New communities devoted to spiritual renewal also emerged. Cursillo, the Catholic Charismatic Renewal, and the Marriage Encounter movement—each with debts to Hispanic-American Catholicism—provided small, intensive, faith community contexts for individuals, married couples, and families. Critics disparaged these movements as symptomatic of Catholics' retreat into privatized pursuits.[60] Others welcomed them as instances of a longstanding Catholic appreciation for *Gemeinschaft*,[61] communal contexts affording personal and spiritual nourishment.

The Future: Treasures and Challenges

The post-Vatican II years destabilized many earlier locaters of U.S. Catholic identity. Yet much endured. Exhibiting an ever-richer palette of cultural variation, U.S. Catholic families fostered religious imaginations steeped in the sacramental dimensions of everyday living. They remained loyal to a venerable and demanding set of religious and moral ideals, and to a capacious ecclesial and pastoral tradition evincing tolerance for the different and the nonideal in people, marriages, and families. Catholics also persevered in a pragmatic, but at times sharply prophetic, religiosity focused on bettering the world, and nourished by profound liturgical roots.

Daunting challenges and unanswered questions confront U.S. Catholic families in the new century. The denouement of transitions originating in the 1960s is yet unknown. Will growing heterogeneity lead to maturing solidarity or to deeper internecine divisions? Will lay ministries, including those of women, be justly integrated with older clerical forms? Can official initiatives toward family-oriented ministry meet families in the places where they really live? What might a seriously embraced theology of family as domestic church imply both for families and for church institutions' internal and public vocations? Concerning such matters, scholars and officials continue to debate and pronounce. But Catholic families, inescapably engaged with the concrete, will provide the proving grounds for the answers.

NOTES

1. Patrick Carey, *The Roman Catholics* (Westport, Conn.: Greenwood Press, 1993), 115.
2. Ibid.
3. Attitudinal polls in the 1980s suggested that, in contrast to the U.S. Protestant worldview, U.S. Catholics were more likely to reconcile reason with faith; to take a more understanding attitude toward sinners and religious diversity; to be intensely concerned with this world; to emphasize social justice as a dimension of faith slightly more than personal piety; and to see religion as an individual choice, thus shying away from active efforts to convert others. George Gallup, Jr., and Jim Castelli, *The American Catholic People: Their Beliefs, Practices, and Values* (Garden City, N.Y.: Doubleday, 1987), 10.
4. Carey, *Roman Catholics,* 111.
5. See Dolores Liptak, *The Catholic Church in the United States: At the Crossroads* (Washington, D.C.: Center for Applied Research in the Apostolate, 1983), 47–54.
6. Ibid., 77.
7. See Jay P. Dolan, R. Scott Appleby, Patricia Byrne, and Debra Campbell, *Transforming Parish Ministry: The Changing Roles of Catholic Clergy, Laity, and Women Religious* (New York: Crossroad, 1989), 297.
8. Between 1940 and 1970, 4 million blacks migrated from rural areas into cities. Bishop Eugene A. Marino, "The Black Family and the American Church," in *Families: Black and Catholic, Catholic and Black,* ed. Thea Bowman (Washington, D.C.: Commission on Marriage and Family Life, USCC, 1985), 73. "In 1940, the country's Hispanic population was 15 percent urban and 85 percent rural; by the early 1950s, those proportions were reversed" (Carol Jensen, "History of the Catholic Parish in the Intermountain West," in *The American Catholic Parish: A History from 1850 to the Present,* vol. 2, ed. Jay P. Dolan [New York: Paulist Press, 1987], 220). See also Cyprian Davis, "Black Catholics: Where? How Many?" in Bowman, *Families: Black and Catholic,* 25–26; Jeffrey Burns, "The Mexican-American Catholic Community," in Dolan, *The American Catholic Parish,* 80; and Moises Sandoval, *On the Move: A History of the Hispanic Church in the United States* (Maryknoll, N.Y.: Orbis Books, 1990), 106–14.

   On racism faced by Hispanic and African American Catholics between

1940 and 1960, see Burns, "The Mexican-American Catholic Community," 85; Carey, *Roman Catholics,* 106–8; John McGreevy, "'Race' and Twentieth Century American Catholic Culture," The Working Paper Series 25, no. 1 (Notre Dame, Ind.: Cushwa Center for the Study of American Catholicism, 1993).

9. Only slowly would the religious styles and gifts of black and Hispanic families begin to be appreciated instead of problematized, thanks to the labors of dedicated clergy and laity such as Jesuit Father John Lafarge with black lay Catholics and Interracial Councils, and those of Catholic Spanish-Speaking Councils. See, for example, Cyprian Davis, *The History of Black Catholics in the United States* (New York: Crossroad, 1990), 225–29; and Moises Sandoval, "The Organization of a Hispanic Church," in *Hispanic Catholic Culture in the U.S.: Issues and Concerns,* ed. Jay P. Dolan and Allen Figueroa Deck (Notre Dame, Ind.: University of Notre Dame Press, 1994), 133–38.

10. In the late 1940s, Catholics in large northern cities ranged from an estimated 22.3 percent in New York City, to 40.8 percent in Chicago, to 67.5 percent in Boston. By 1957, 45 percent of the population in the northeastern states, and 37.8 percent of the population in all large urban areas, identified themselves as Catholic. See McGreevy, "'Race' and American Catholic Culture," 31, n. 6.

11. Dolan, "The 1940s," in Dolan et al., *Transforming Parish Ministry,* 288.

12. On the influence of the theology of the Mystical Body of Christ on U.S. Catholic laity between 1929 and 1959, see Debra Campbell, "The Heyday of Catholic Action and the Lay Apostolate, 1929–1959," in Dolan et al., *Transforming Parish Ministry,* 222–52.

13. The secondary aims of marriage were taught to be the mutual aid and comfort of the spouses—especially aid in reaching their supernatural destinies, and the quieting of concupiscence. See Pope Pius XII, "The Apostolate of the Midwife," 1951, in *Papal Pronouncements on Marriage and the Family from Leo XIII to Pius XII (1878–1954),* ed. Alvin Werth and Clement S. Mihanovich (Milwaukee: Bruce Publishing Company, 1955), 63.

14. Pope Pius XI, *"Casti Connubii,* Christian Marriage in Our Day," 1930, no. 14, in *Social Wellsprings,* vol. 2, ed. Joseph Husslein (Milwaukee: Bruce Publishing, Company, 1942), 130.

15. Typical topics were conditions for lawful sexual pleasure and intercourse in marriage, and condemnations of artificial birth control, sterilization, abortion, artificial insemination, and "the evil of unhallowed marriage" (Ibid., 56–117, 118–53); also Lisa Sowle Cahill, "Catholic Sexual Ethics and the Dignity of the Person: A Double Message," *Theological Studies* 50 (March 1989):120–50.

16. This does not mean, says Pius XI, that a wife should obey her husband's requests if they contravene right reason or the dignity due her; nor does it imply that wives should be treated or considered as legal minors. Pope Pius XI, *"Casti Connubii,* Christian Marriage in Our Day," 1930, no. 27, in Husslein, *Social Wellsprings,* 134.

17. Ibid.

18. Pius XII, "Woman's Duties in Social and Political Life," 1945, in Werth and Mihanovich, *Papal Pronouncements,* 44.

19. In 1956, for instance, the progressive Christian Family Movement adopted an insignia that represented "Man, Woman, and Child as a Family United in Christ." The symbol for man, an upward Y, and for woman a downward Y, were explained: "Man: Shown with arms lifted up to God, standing as a tower of great strength, which exemplifies his place as head of the family." "Woman: Reaching toward the earth in her fertility—the place she holds in the divine plan of creation, fulfilled in the family unit" (Martin Quigley, Jr., and Monsignor Edward M. Connors, *Catholic Action in Practice: Family Life, Education, International Life* [New York: Random House, 1963], 156–57).

20. Mary Reed Newland, *We and Our Children: Molding the Child in Christian Living* (Garden City, N.Y.: Doubleday, [1954] 1961). The book, by 1961 in its seventh printing, synthesized common sense, contemporary child psychology, popularized presentations of church teaching, and middle-class Euro-American Catholic piety. Its cover depicts a mother reading a book to her seven children, who lovingly surround her. Compare with n. 59, below.

21. Newland suggests that a mother tell her young child, "[W]henever he is tempted to indulge in this pleasure which God forbids, he can fold his hands together tightly, like this, and quick as a wink say inside himself, 'Please, Blessed Mother, help me to be pure.' She will, because she is so pure herself and she loves purity so much. She knows all about little children and how hard things can go for them. She will send all the grace he needs, as soon as he needs it, if only he will ask her. She will watch over him, with God, and she will be pleased when he is successful (though of course just as sad when he is not)" (Ibid., 113).

22. The priority of family was evident also in accepted behavior at Mass. Newland reports attending Mass as a child in a small Mexican-American town. Mothers brought their babies with them, set them in the aisle, "and Mass was heard over a chorus of howls, chirps and yammers. No one seemed to mind the noise, nor the puddles in the aisle afterwards" (Ibid., 129).

23. For the Hispanic Catholic child, "The greater part of one's faith life and devotional life is learned from mothers and grandmothers who make use of novenas, prayers, and *imagenes* to communicate the religious sense and to foster a personal and family spirituality. This whole strain of religiosity has been developed without the need for the presence of priests and is generally unrelated to the official liturgical life of the Church" (Burns, "The Mexican-American Catholic Community," 86–87, citing Rev. Rigoberto Calcoa-Rivas, "U.S. Hispanics and the Catholic Church," *The Oakland Catholic Voice,* September 26, 1983, 18).

24. Jensen, "History of the Catholic Parish," 212. On *padrinzgo* (godparenting) and *compadrazgo* (literally coparenting), and the deeply rooted sense of family and collectivism among Hispanic Catholics, see Isidoro Lucas, *The Browning of America: The Hispanic Revolution in the American Church*

(Chicago: Fides/Claretian Books, 1981), 58–60. Lucas suggests that the relatively few priestly vocations among Hispanic Catholics may be traced to a model of celibate priesthood "that focused on severing and transcending all family ties" (Ibid., 42–43).

25. Richard Rodriguez recalls his mother telling him that the Mexican Mary "honored our people" by choosing to "appear to a Mexican, someone like us." "And she appeared, I could see from her picture, as a young Indian maiden—dark just like me" (quoted in Burns, "The Mexican-American Catholic Community," in Dolan, *The American Catholic Parish*, 86).

26. Ibid.

27. Wade W. Nobles, "African American Family Life: An Instrument of Culture," in *Black Families,* ed. Harriet Pipes McAdoo(Newbury Park, Calif.: Sage Publications, 1988), 46. John U. Ogbu identifies four features of "caste-like minorities": they have been incorporated into "their country" involuntarily and permanently; membership is acquired permanently at birth; they have more limited access to the social goods of society by virtue of their group membership; they tend to focus on their economic and social problems in terms of collective institutional discrimination, which they perceive as more than temporary. "Black Education: A Cultural-Ecological Perspective," in *Black Families,* 174.

28. The Christocentric piety of 1950s black Catholic families is suggested by Shawn Copeland's early childhood memory of her great–grandmother's explanation of the devotional picture prominently displayed on her bedroom wall: "This is Jesus. He died for us. He loves us." See also note 25 above.

29. In Chicago, for example, black parishioners of Corpus Christi staged an annual outdoor "living stations of the Cross" that attracted thousands between 1937 and 1968. *Corpus Christi Parish, Our History, 1901–1977* (Chicago: Privately printed, 1977), cited by Shaw in Dolan, *The American Catholic Parish*, 379, n. 2.

30. Carey, *Roman Catholics,* 94.

31. Ibid., 101–6; Campbell, "The Heyday of Catholic Action," in Dolan et al., *Transforming Parish Ministry,* 222–52.

32. Some regarded this development positively, as preparing the way for post-Vatican II lay involvement, but others criticized the contradictory internal-external thrusts of CFM and Cana and their lack of integration into parish life. See Msgr. George A. Kelly, *The Battle for the American Church* (Garden City, N.Y.: Image, 1981), 213–14, cited by R. Scott Appleby, in Dolan et al., *Transforming Parish Ministry,* 49.

33. Carey, *Roman Catholics,* 95, 198–99. On the CFM, see Jeffrey Burns, "The Christian Family Movement," The Working Paper Series 11, no. 2 (Notre Dame, Ind.: Cushwa Center for the Study of American Catholicism, Spring 1982); Quigley and Connors, *Catholic Action in Practice,* 111–68; Campbell, in Dolan et al., *Transforming Parish Ministry,* 248–50, 256–57, 263–64. On Cana Conferences, see ibid., 248–50. At its peak in the early 1960s, the CFM comprised over 10,000 couples, whose small chapters

met in homes—usually with a priest-chaplain present—to pray, study inquiry materials on family and social matters, discuss and plan social actions, and socialize. Quigley and Connors, *Catholic Action,* 111–12. Cana Conference programs were adopted by many dioceses and, in the 1990s, continued to facilitate marriage preparation (Pre-Cana) and retreats for married couples. See *Official Catholic Directory 1991* (Wilmette, Ill.: P.J. Kenedy & Sons, 1991), A-45.

34. Carey, *Roman Catholics,* 95.

35. Davis, *History of Black Catholics,* 236–37.

36. See Carey, *Roman Catholics,* 120.

37. In 1984, Catholics comprised 44 percent of the population in the eastern U.S., 26 percent in the midwest, 16 percent in the south, and 26 percent in the west. See Gallup and Castelli, *American Catholic People,* 2–6; Carey, *Roman Catholics,* 119–22; and *Official Catholic Directory 1991,* 1–40.

38. By 1987, one in five Catholics belonged to minority groups. Eleven million were Hispanics (16 percent), two million were black (3 percent), and another two million described themselves as "nonwhite," including native Americans and growing numbers of Catholics of southeast Asian origin. By contrast, among Protestants, 14 percent were black and 2 percent Hispanic. Gallup and Castelli, *American Catholic People,* 3.

39. Todd David Whitmore, "Children and the Problem of Formation in American Families," *Annual of the Society of Christian Ethics,* 1995, 263–74, discusses these shifts for women and their impact on childrearing from a Roman Catholic perspective. Cf. Christine Firer Hinze, "Women and Families," in ibid., 275–86.

40. See Gallup and Castelli, *American Catholic People,* 59–65, 103–15; Andrew Greeley, *American Catholics Since the Council: An Unauthorized Report* (Chicago, Ill.: The Thomas More Press, 1985), 80–100, 181–92.

41. These developments were symbolized by the issuance of two pastoral letters, "The Hispanic Presence: Challenge and Commitment" (Washington, D.C.: National Council of Catholic Bishops, 1983), and "What We Have Seen and Heard: A Pastoral Letter on Evangelization from the Black Bishops of the United States" (Washington, D.C.: National Council of Catholic Bishops, 1984). Also illustrative is the self-consciously diverse collage of family photographs adorning *Families in the '80s: Family Decade Resource for Community, Diocese and Parish* (Washington, D.C.: U.S. Catholic Conference Commission on Marriage and Family Life, 1980).

42. Gallup and Castelli, *American Catholic People,* 5.

43. Dolan et al., *Transforming Parish Ministry,* 309.

44. In 1963, 44 percent of Catholic children were in parochial schools; by 1974, the proportion had dropped by one-third to 29 percent. Eleven of those fifteen percentage points were concentrated in suburban areas (Greeley, *American Catholics,* 167). Greeley's studies suggested that, compared with parochial school attendance, other religious education formats had little positive impact on adult religious attitudes and behaviors (Ibid., 171).

45. See, for example, "Constitution on the Church in the Modern World," #48 and #50, in *The Documents of Vatican II,* ed. Walter M. Abbott (New York: Guild Press, 1966), 250–55.

46. Pope John Paul II, *Familiaris Consortio.* Papal Exhortation on the Family (Washington, D.C.: USCC Office of Publishing and Promoting Services, 1981), #21.

47. See Ad Hoc Committee on Marriage and Family Life, *A Family Perspective in Church and Society* (Washington, D.C.: National Conference of Catholic Bishops, 1987).

48. Ibid., 19. Compare U.S. Catholic Bishops, "Putting Children and Families First: A Challenge for Our Church, Nation, and World," *Origins* 21/25 (29 November 1991), 404, n.1.

49. See *Lumen Gentium* 11, in Abbott, *Documents of Vatican II,* 29.

50. See *A Family Perspective,* 21–22, citing Pope John Paul II, *Familiaris Consortio,* #49.

51. Ibid., Introduction and passim.

52. See Pope John XXIII, *Pacem in Terris,* #41; cited in Maria Riley, "Women," in *The New Dictionary of Catholic Social Thought,* ed. Judith Dwyer (Collegeville, Minn.: Liturgical Press, 1994), 986–91.

53. Pope John Paul II, *Laborem Exercens,* On Human Work (Washington, D.C.: Daughters of St. Paul, 1981), #19.

54. Perhaps in deference to the degree of support for women's equal status across the U.S. Catholic community, official pronouncements of the American bishops, though never rebutting the pope's proposals concerning gender differences, have declined to underscore them.

55. An excellent overview of Catholic social teaching on families, with special attention to its treatment of women, is Margaret A. Farley, "Family," in Dwyer, *New Dictionary of Catholic Social Thought,* 371–81.

56. Weekly Mass attendance was recorded at 74 percent in 1958, underwent a steep decline between 1969 and 1975, and stabilized at about 52 percent by 1985 (13 percent higher than church attendance by Protestants). See Gallup and Castelli, *American Catholic People,* 26–32.

57. Greeley, *American Catholics,* 198–206.

58. Ibid., 70.

59. James and Kathleen McGinnis, cofounders of the network, wrote a widely read manual on integrating family life, spirituality, and social action, *Parenting for Peace and Justice* (Maryknoll, N.Y.: Orbis Press, 1980, 1990). Comparing this text (whose cover features a mother, father, and three children gazing into the horizon together, and a photo of the authors' multiracial family) with Newland's (n. 20, above) provides a graphic illustration of differences between popular 1950s and 1980s Euro-American Catholic family spiritualities and lifeworlds.

60. See Campbell in Dolan et al., *Transforming Parish Ministry,* 265–66.

61. Compare with Greeley, *American Catholics,* 261.

5

African Methodist Episcopal: Nurturing a Sense of "Somebodyness"

WILLIAM P. DEVEAUX

The African Methodist Episcopal (AME) church was born of protest. Founded in 1816 to combat persecution, the problems it faced then seem to parallel problems inherent in life in twentieth-century America. Then, as now, the urgency for African Methodism was redemption of society rather than strict emphasis upon theological doctrine. For the early AMEs, redemption meant changing their condition of servitude to becoming full participants as citizens in America. Black worshipers endured for many years being relegated to seats in the church gallery. When they, however, were denied the opportunity to pray at the altar of St. George's Methodist Episcopal Church in Philadelphia and were forcibly ejected for trying to do so, Richard Allen, Absalom Jones, and forty-two followers walked out in protest and established the Free African Society. Its mission was to provide charity for the bereaved, the widowed, and the orphaned; to educate adults as well as children; and to promote cooperative savings plans among Society members. The Free African Society was the forerunner of the AME denomination, and its first church, Mother Bethel, was housed in Allen's blacksmith shop.

African Methodists within contemporary American society borrow from the creativity exhibited by Allen and his followers. They insist on providing a nurturing place where families can grow and where persons can develop a sense of "somebodyness." To be somebody, for black Americans, is to be self-actualized, and to understand one's place in the grand scheme of God's divine plan. The AME basis of theology is that the people under its auspices are "somebody" simply because God created them. Often preachers will paraphrase passages in Psalm 8:5, "God has made us a little lower than the angels and crowned us with glory and honor." Thus, to be "somebody" for black Americans is to fully understand that God has made them in God's own image.

To analyze the family and the African Methodist Episcopal church, it is important to appreciate how other black denominations approach this issue as well. Although African Methodists are unique in many ways, they also have much in common with other black denominations. As Andrew Billingsley points out in his recent book *Climbing Jacob's Ladder,* "It is a mistake to think of the black church in America as simply, or even primarily, a religious institution in the same way the white church might be conceived."[1]

The black church has historically been much more than a place of Christian fellowship and worship. Historian C. Eric Lincoln and sociologist Lawrence H. Mamiya describe a gathering of family and extended families "worshiping in a sanctuary they themselves erected and burying their dead in the church yards that were already hallowed by memories of past generations it enshrined." The black family is in their view "the primary unit of the black church," and they see a symbiosis between family and church "which makes for mutual reinforcement and creates for most black families their initial, or primary, identity."[2]

For over 200 years the African Methodist Episcopal Church has challenged and fought the enemies of justice and freedom. It has affirmed and defended the rights of black people and has sought to give a sense of dignity and identity to people who have been abused and neglected. Its scope of concern continues to be as broad as the Christian religion itself. The motto of the AME church, "God our Father, Christ our Redeemer, Man our Brother," indicates that the church defines its mission in familial terms. As the twenty-first century dawns, it is evident that much work is left to be done and, more important, much is still expected of the church. The black family's composition has changed radically and a sense of urgency has emerged. The AME church and its members must find ways to meet the needs of the changing family structure and to bring hope to persons who are in despair.

The Historical Perspective

In the African Methodist tradition, the family is a primary and essential unit in both the local and the national church. The definition of a family for African Methodists and indeed to all black Americans, is not limited to husband, wife, and offspring, but includes everyone living under a single roof. Therefore, the relationship between church and family is a tightly woven bond that spans generations and is committed to addressing social ills that affect not only its members but society in general. According to Billingsley, it is "at the leading edge of the African American community's push to influence the future of its families."[3]

When the AME church was established, it was organized primarily as a burial society to care for the bereaved and ensure that persons were buried with dignity. Richard Allen and a group of black men and women responded to the needs of their people by later establishing the Free African Society. As the forerunner of the African Methodist Episcopal Church, the Free African Society tackled social issues and emphasized family pride, self-help, dignity, and human development. Many of those colonial concerns still face contemporary black Americans and are among the issues that the church must now address.

Slavery and Reconstruction

The AME church is accustomed to dealing with radical changes in American society. It supported its members through that "peculiar institution," slavery—the most ruthless form of human servitude ever known. Over a period of 300 years, men and women were kidnapped from the continent of Africa and enslaved in America. Overcoming this form of servitude called for a great exhibition of human resiliency. When slavery ended, African Methodists worked with other black Christians to sustain the hopes of African Americans through the difficult Reconstruction period. The church served as a "balm in Gilead" during an era in which the Ku Klux Klan and "night riders" enforced the black segregation codes. It sought to bring dignity to black people when the courts of the land mandated that they had no rights that white America was obliged to uphold. Billingsley explains that its "genius" was centered in complete ownership and control by African Americans: "It represented freedom, independence and respect for its leadership, as well as the opportunity for self-esteem, self-development, leadership and relaxation. Moreover, they found that the black church was a community and recreational center that encouraged education, business development and democratic fellowship beyond its members."[4]

In the early days of the twentieth century, African Methodists such as the Reverend Reverdy Cassius Ransom became sources of inspiration for the emerging civil rights struggle. It was Ransom, later a bishop in the AME church, who, by force of his oratorical brilliance, maintained the Niagara Movement, which subsequently evolved into what is now the National Association for the Advancement of Colored People.

The Postwar Era

The period immediately following World War II was an especially pivotal time of transition in black families. The black exodus from the south accelerated as black Americans left a hostile but familiar environment below the Mason-Dixon line to pursue jobs in the more-tolerant industrial cities of the north. The black church assisted in the migration of blacks into the northern cities and to the west coast, where the postwar economy continued to flourish. As they had during the Depression, the clergy and laity formed networks that became primary sources of employment and housing for African Methodists during periods of transition, providing needed insight and direction amid unfamiliar surroundings.

To cope with the demands of these new city dwellers, churches developed new social policies and innovative programming. Many churches stayed open seven days a week to provide spiritual power and a place of refuge. In addition, day-care facilities, after-school programs, and evening activities became essential elements of church life. Churches provided these services because black families had become dependent on the incomes of all adults in the home. Fathers, mothers, and older siblings worked long hours, often at some distance from home. In these situations, the church met the increased familial need for a strong support base that was safe and convenient.

The Civil Rights Years

African Methodists have been involved in every stage of the struggle for human rights. In the late 1950s and 1960s, at the height of the civil rights movement, the AME churches provided stopping places and reservoirs of support for people who were fighting for social justice. For example, Brown Chapel African Methodist Episcopal Church in Selma, Alabama, was the starting point for the famous march led by Martin Luther King, Jr., across the Edmund Pettis Bridge.

The civil rights struggle had both immediate and far-reaching consequences for black families. The 1954 Supreme Court decision of *Brown v. Board of Education* mandated that children would be bussed to schools outside their neighborhoods in an effort to end segregation. Black family life was irrevocably changed. Children were no longer a part of their neighborhood schools. As a result, parents or other family members were often unable to visit the school in support of their children's school activities. Black pastors, Sunday School superintendents and concerned members of congregations often functioned as surrogate parents, attending Parent-Teacher Association meetings and sporting events when family members were unavailable. Accountable only to the churches that paid their salaries, pastors were able to visit throughout the community without fear of reprisal from white employers. Such independence gave pastors the freedom to fight against racism as a presence within an often alien education system; to support and uplift struggling black children in an often predominantly white and racist environment.

It was Bethel African Methodist Episcopal Church in Little Rock, Arkansas, that provided sustenance for Ernest Green, the student leader of the "Little Rock Nine" that integrated Little Rock's Central High School. Under the leadership of its pastor, the Reverend R. K. Young, Bethel African Methodist Episcopal Church became a supportive extended family. In this way, the pastor and congregation fulfilled the mandate to advocate social justice, as well as to be family for a young man who needed their encouragement to complete his studies and, more important, to cope with the problems of adapting to a newly integrated school.

The AME church and other black churches, though vigilant in the struggle against all forms of racism, often appeared more capable of dealing with overt racism than with the subtleties of segregation in the post–civil rights era. Segregationists and conservatives found new and creative means of restricting the movement of blacks within society. Breaking housing covenants that restricted black access to certain areas of the city and crashing the "glass ceiling" in the workplace became the new battlegrounds. The black church had to formulate strategies to address family units and individuals in dealing with a dream that was seriously deferred.

Lyndon Johnson's Great Society program also had an enormous impact on both the black family and the black church. The Head Start program, which dramatically improved educational opportunities for millions of black children, was perhaps the most significant initiative in President Johnson's antipoverty campaign. However, it brought negative consequences as well. In all too many instances churches reverted from being primary service providers to becoming referral agents for their members. Certainly not all black churches eliminated their outreach programs, but enough did to make an acute problem. The church placed greater emphasis on directing persons to social aid agencies than on providing needed assistance at church locations. Pastors and church leaders often became involved in poverty programs where they sought to demand rights from the government rather than putting their energies into making the church a place in which these services were rendered.

An additional problem resulted from the antipoverty programs of the 1960s and, indeed, in the years that followed; one that is now debated by psychologists and sociologists. Many argue that government programs such as Aid to Families with Dependent Children have fundamentally altered the black family unit. Because such programs focus on the needs of mothers, many fathers have played a decreased role in raising their children.

The African Methodist Response to an Ever-Evolving Definition of Family

As the AME church moves into the twenty-first century, it is challenged to a new level of understanding in its relationship to the family. Blacks have been redefining the essence of familial relationships since their arrival in this country in 1619. Slavery, Reconstruction, and the "Black Diaspora" have brought forth innovative ways of dealing with family issues. However, the problems facing the church and its relationship to the family unit in the 1990s can, at times, make the family problems faced in the past seem almost trivial. The AME church must continue to affirm families of all types, configurations, and conditions while providing alternate means to serve these children of God.

Non-"Traditional" Family Configurations

Family life has changed radically since the postwar years. The percentage of blacks living in what has been called "traditional" families has decreased substantially, and many blacks have been raised in single-parent homes. A recent survey reported, "More than fifty percent of all black families are headed by single women, while the problem of teen pregnancy, crime, substance abuse, illiteracy, family dissolution and unemployment are at an all time high. Solutions to the crises of these families are being generated in the entire black community and through the Black church."[5] In 1992, a commission established by the Annie E. Casey Foundation in Baltimore reported that

> one in four children or 19 percent of the youngsters in the United States lived in single-parent homes headed by mothers. Of that

number a whopping 36 percent of those children were living in poverty compared to only 7 percent of children living in two-parent homes. In the black community, the statistics are even more staggering. For in the same year, the number of households headed by mothers reached well over 50 percent. And sadly, among those children, 73 percent lived below the poverty line.[6]

Susan B. Newman in her recent work, *With Heart and Hand: The Black Church Working to Save Black Children,* has indicated that

> we have many problems to solve—every forty-six seconds of the school day, a black child drops out of school, every sixty-five seconds, a black teenager becomes sexually active, every one hundred and four seconds, a black teenage girl becomes pregnant, every eleven minutes, a black child is arrested for a violent crime and every twenty hours, a black child, or young adult under twenty-five, dies from causes related to HIV.[7]

Newman goes on to suggest that although these facts can be daunting, they also should serve as the inspiration for positive action.

Some AME church leaders have responded to these challenges with a deeper sense of social mission. The Reverend Cecil L. "Chip" Murray of First African Methodist Episcopal Church, Los Angeles, and his congregation, have demonstrated how the philosophy of AME church founder Richard Allen is employed in contemporary America. Murray told Iris Schneider of the *Los Angeles Times,* "If we don't change the community, the community will corrupt the individual." He continued, "the coming to church for personal salvation days are over. Now we are looking not only for personal salvation, but for social salvation."[8] Thus as a recent study of black churches reports, Murray has led his church from a membership of some 300 from his appointment in 1977 to over 7,500 by the end of 1991. Murray attributes this growth "to the philosophy and activity of the church in reaching 'beyond the walls' of the church into a massive array of community outreach programs."[9]

Men: The Compelling Challenge Now and for the Twenty-First Century

Weakened family structures are pervasive in today's America—particularly among black families. Government aid has solved one problem while creating another: the absent father. No sincere effort was made by government agencies to provide financial support for families who sought to maintain a two-parent household. Instead, black men and women found themselves losing government benefits once they found new jobs. In addition, women were able to receive additional funding for an increased number of children. Such government funding, though not an incentive to bear more children, has certainly allowed the practice to become more acceptable within a wide segment of impoverished America. It has also created a disincentive for men to remain with their children. There is a price to be exacted for accepting government aid.

The 1990s are seeing a new and significant focus to the work done by the AME church in America: the reclamation of the black male. This, according to Bishop Philip R. Cousin, must be the number one concern of the black family. As chair of the AME Church General Board in 1993, he argued that the black male must be brought back into the mainstream of church life. Congregations need to understand that in order to have a fully functional family one must have a strong black male presence.[10] Bishop Cousin insisted that any emphasis on black manhood need not jeopardize the status of black women. "We are trying to catch up and bring the black male up to the status where the black female has positioned herself through years of work, dedication and sometimes as the stable member of the household," he argued. "But in the attempt to bring the black male forward, we must make certain that we do not isolate the black female. We have to lock them both arm-in-arm, hand-in-hand and spirit-to-spirit and make sure we have a total family unit."[11]

The importance of black women in African-American church life is indisputable. Research has indicated that 78 percent of black women respond that they pray daily, outnumbering men in this activity 84 percent to 68 percent. Further, 71 percent indicated that they attend church with some regularity, or at least once a month, again outnumbering men by 76 percent to 61 percent. In addition, 68 percent of black women listen to weekly religious broadcasts, and 50 percent read religious books and other religious materials weekly (substantially outnumbering men in all of these activities).[12] How can this be explained? As noted historian and author Herbert W. Toler, Jr., suggests, "The fact that black men seem to have a strong set of religious beliefs, but do not convert these into practice as frequently as women do, raises questions about the structure of society, or the structure of the church, that restrains men's religious participation."[13] Churches may well need to reevaluate their organizational structures, Toler warns, if they are determined to reclaim black males to membership.

The empowerment of men and their place in the church has caused some tension within the AME church and the entire African-American religious community. But the battle for participation by black men must go on. In his book, *Upon This Rock,* The Reverend Johnnie Ray Young-blood of the St. Paul Community Baptist Church in Brooklyn, New York, contends emphatically that activities at most churches are not designed with the interests and talents of men in mind, and he has begun a "male ministry" to correct that oversight.[14]

Likewise, The Reverend Dr. Frank M. Reid III, pastor of Bethel African Methodist Episcopal Church in Baltimore, Maryland, has established a ministry to men called "Mighty Men of God" (MMOG). It is based on the belief that the black church and the black family will be saved when men return to positions of responsibility. Training for participation in MMOG emphasizes devotion to God and the community, discipline within self and church, spiritual development, and social deliverance, both individually and institutionally. Each man is encouraged to be the leader of his family and the spiritual head of his house. Reid is mindful of the potential danger that the black male's newly found assertive nature would be misinterpreted by the black female. To forestall this, Reid's ministry to men includes working with women to restore male authority in the home. "Men will be better fathers and husbands and will participate more willingly in church and community life," he argues, "if they are allowed to exercise authority as head of the household." He stresses that "this does not mean tyranny or dictatorial control, but rather loving responsibility." Each man is taught "to be the protector, priest, provider and partner of the household." He further notes that "the Old Testament instructs the man to be 'watchman for his family'."[15]

The concept of a men's ministry is operating in most AME churches. At Metropolitan African Methodist Episcopal Church in Washington, D.C., the "Mighty Men of Valour" serve as the "male muscle" for the church. The men are first empowered by prayer and Christian fellowship. They then serve in every area of church life, often providing the physical as well as the spiritual "muscle" to get things done. The men's ministry provides security for the church, transportation for the elderly, and support services for all youth activities, but their most important purpose is to act as role models to the entire church family.

Programs similar to MMOG and the "Mighty Men of Valour" are being developed at regional and national church levels. In each instance, men's concerns are emphasized. Establishing programs for and in consultation with men requires reconfiguring some current church practices and structures so that men will realize that they are encouraged to participate in church activities. The result has been a steady return of black men to the church.

Effective Parenting

Effective parenting also receives special attention in the AME church. The statistics concerning single-parent homes and the pressure placed on black families has made focusing on parenting skills a high priority for black churches. Parenting programs found at Bridge Street African Methodist Episcopal Church, Brooklyn, New York, and at Bethel African Methodist Episcopal Church in Baltimore, Maryland, have proved to be extremely effective in providing strength for families in crisis. The programs also include a broad range of support to single- and two-parent families, who come mostly from a poor or working class background. These programs promote such activities as Big Brother, Big Sister, Foster Grandparents, and Family Crisis Intervention. With a paid staff of five, these programs are financed by state and local funds, as well as by contributions from the churches involved.

At Bethel, parenting skills efforts are directed at teenage parents. The Teen Parenting Enrichment Place was formed in 1992 to prevent adolescent pregnancy and to enhance the parenting skills of both male and female teen parents. This multiservice support center is financed by the church and the state government to provide assistance to teen parents, their children, and the children's grandparents. Programs that deal with parenting, although less developed and on a smaller scale, can be found in most AME churches. Parenting is an issue that unites all segments of the community, though focusing on men and their relationship to the family.

In his latest study, Andrew Billingsley has confirmed that black churches are extremely family oriented. In a study of the northeastern United States, he found family-oriented community outreach programs in seven out of ten churches. He concluded that the church has the potential to unite the black community—upper class, middle class, working class, and poor—in assisting poor families to regain hope for the future. Billingsley's affirmation of the black church's activities is set against the backdrop of skepticism he has encountered from those who doubt that the black church can correct the ills related to the family. "Americans would do well to remember the black church has a track record," Billingsley points out. "While there is a certain amount of skepticism in the nation about the capacity of the black churches to coalesce around the priority issues, the long-term research reported on has established . . . that some two-thirds . . . of black churches in the study are already actively involved in family-oriented community outreach programs at the local level," he adds, and "the overwhelming majority are disposed to cooperative arrangements with nonreligious community agencies as well."[16]

Wallace Charles Smith, the pastor of the inner city Shiloh Baptist Church, Washington, D.C., suggests "a cooperative strategy" between the church and the community on behalf of black families. Smith urges a realistic approach that would recognize the historic role of the black church as a suffering community, a community of extended families, an inclusive community, an adoptionist community, and, finally, a hopeful community.[17] Such experiments continue the legacy of the black church, which throughout its history has broadened its mission in response to the needs of its members. As Benjamin Mays and Joseph Nicholson observed over half a century ago, despite its problems and failures "there is in the genius or the 'soul' of the [black] church something that gives it life and vitality, that makes it stand out significantly above its buildings, creeds, rituals and doctrines, something that makes it a unique institution."[18]

Conclusion

An overview of the AME church's approach to family-related issues since 1945 reveals that its primary role, although slightly modified, is still essentially the same. The church provides a stronghold for its members. It is on the one hand a "refuge in a time of storm" whereas on the other hand it provides a "battle axe in a time of war." In the AME church many sermons are preached on themes concerning enclaves of security ("My God Is a Rock in a Weary Land"). Sermons proclaim the radicality of God's demand for justice: "The Spirit of the LORD is upon Me, Because He has anointed Me to preach the gospel to the poor. . . . To set at liberty those who are oppressed, To preach the acceptable year of the LORD" (Luke 4:18–19, NKJV).

The AME church has provided for the survival of the family and has created new opportunities for its prosperity. Survival means the black family staying together and understanding that, individually and collectively, family units can strive for excellence and can grow. A step beyond survival, prosperity encompasses many aspects of the human experience: economic stability, social acceptability, and professional opportunities.

The AME church continues to provide a place of sanctuary while preparing black families to cope with and to surmount challenges posed by a predominantly white culture. For this reason, the AME definition of family is neither proscriptive nor coercive. It acknowledges the typical family while embracing all manner of human relationships within this unit.

NOTES

1. Andrew Billingsley, *Climbing Jacob's Ladder: The Enduring Legacy of African-American Families* (New York: Simon & Schuster, 1992), 352.
2. C. Eric Lincoln and Lawrence H. Mamiya, *The Black Church in the African Experience* (Durham, N.C.: Duke University Press, 1990), 402.
3. Billingsley, *Climbing Jacob's Ladder,* 350.
4. Ibid., 354.
5. Kim A. Lawton, "Giving Black Families a Boost," *Christianity Today,* 13 August 1991, 19.
6. *Jet,* 29 May 1995, 14.
7. Susan D. Newman, *With Heart and Hand: The Black Church Working to Save Black Children* (Valley Forge: Judson Press, 1994), vii.
8. Billingsley, *Climbing Jacob's Ladder,* 350.
9. Ibid., 351.
10. *Ebony,* August 1993, 95.
11. Ibid.
12. Billingsley, *Climbing Jacob's Ladder,* 356.
13. Herbert H. Toler, Jr., "Fisher of Men," *Policy Review* (Spring 1995):76.
14. The Reverend Johnnie Ray Youngblood, as quoted in Billingsley, *Climbing Jacob's Ladder,* 356.
15. Ibid., 360.
16. Ibid., 377.
17. Wallace Charles Smith, *The Church in the Life of the Black Family* (Valley Forge: Judson Press, 1985), 14.
18. Benjamin E. Mays and Joseph Nicholson, *The Negro's Church* (New York: Institute of Social and Religious Research, 1933; reprint New York: Arno Press/New York Times, 1969), 278.

6

Methodist:
'Tis Grace Will
Lead Us Home

JEAN MILLER SCHMIDT
GAIL E. MURPHY-GEISS

John and Charles Wesley, the founders of the Methodist movement in England, grew up and were nurtured in the Christian faith in a rather remarkable eighteenth-century household. Their father, Samuel, was a scholarly priest in the Church of England who for most of his life served a remote rural parish in Epworth. Their mother, Susanna, was unusually well educated for her day, having been taught by her father, Dr. Samuel Annesley. Both parents were the children of nonconformist (Puritan) ministers, but both had converted as young adults to the Established Church. Susanna gave birth to seventeen children, ten of whom survived to adulthood. She provided these seven girls and three boys with a basic education, as well as formation in the Christian faith. A woman of strong mind and independent conscience, Susanna Wesley undoubtedly had a positive influence on the way women were regarded in the early Methodist movement.

The Wesleyan Tradition:
"Universal Love, Not Confined"[1]

John Wesley spent most of his life struggling to define and refine his theology, but for the purposes of this discussion of family, three main themes are important. The first is his emphasis on grace, which he developed in response to the Calvinist doctrine of predestination. Instead of the view that redemption was only for the "elect" (those chosen), Wesley believed that God's grace was given to all, so that all who responded in faith might attain salvation. The second is his stress on experience as evidence of God's action in the world. Wesley was always willing to accept the lived testimony of others (tested by Scripture and reason), even when it opposed the traditional teachings of the church. The best example of this was his acceptance of women as Methodist class leaders and (a few) lay preachers, based on his conviction that their Christian service was to be judged by its fruits rather than by strictures that might limit the workings of the Holy Spirit. Third, Wesley taught that God's love was universal, so that Christians were not to restrict their love to those with whom they agreed, to next door neighbors, friends, or family. A Christian was to love all people.

In this all-encompassing acceptance, Wesley provided the foundation for the present diversity in the United Methodist Church.[2] It is not possible to describe United Methodists as poor or rich, liberal or conservative, southern or northern, eastern or western, North American or global, for in a very real sense, they are everyone. This Wesleyan theological mixture of the availability of grace, the validity of experience, and the universality of God's love made for a basic commitment to openness and pluralism that has remained central to Methodists throughout history, influencing how they see everything, including the family.

Methodism was brought to North America in the 1760s by emigrating Methodist lay families such as those of Robert and Elizabeth Strawbridge in Maryland, and Philip and Mary Embury and Barbara and Paul Heck in New York. Especially after the organization of the Methodist Episcopal Church as a separate denomination in 1784, Methodist leadership shifted to the typically celibate, male itinerant preachers who served under the authority and followed the example of their bishop, Francis Asbury. Women were excluded from these ranks but played important roles in the countercultural Methodist movement by converting family members and friends, starting churches, and giving leadership as spiritual "mothers" and "sisters," working side by side with the lonely and exhausted traveling clergy. Almost as soon as Asbury died in 1816, the itinerant preachers began to marry these inspiring women, and like many Methodists, moved west as families following the frontier.

By the mid-nineteenth century, American Methodism encouraged a community of spiritual equality and kinship in which Methodist people were to be the "family of God" over against the values and temptations of "the world." The family became a "crucible of moral influence" in which the mother's role was to cultivate evangelical faith, Christian virtue, and responsible citizenship.[3] The Methodist life of faith was to be one of both personal and social holiness, practiced in works of private piety and neighborliness, as well as in commitment to the alleviation of social evils. Rituals of family worship undergirded these values and contributed to the separation and protection of domestic life from worldly influences. This pattern would shape Methodist views of the family for generations to come.

Even when told that their appropriate place was in the home, Methodist women struggled to find ways to respond to their call to serve God. Women of color and poor white women rarely had the privilege of choosing between work and home. White middle-class women found that participating in women's religious voluntary societies helped to expand the boundaries of their "proper" sphere. Some women became ministers' wives, and others experienced a call to preach and became traveling evangelists. By the 1880s, women began to try to make the world more "homelike" by moving into more public work through organizations such as the Woman's Christian Temperance Union and women's foreign and home missionary societies. Although a few women in the smaller predecessor bodies of what is now the United Methodist Church were ordained in the 1880s and 1890s, the vast majority of Methodist women had to wait until the mid-twentieth century for ordination. Their ideal place was still the home, and their presence there as wives and mothers defined the ideal family. Reality, however, did not always match this model. Even as the ideal was being expressed, the forms of Methodist families were transformed and transforming.

1945–1960:
"Together in the Home"[4]

In 1956, the Methodist Church inaugurated a new magazine. Called *Together,* it was to be a "midmonth magazine for Methodist families." In the first issue, October 1956, the editors explained its purpose. It would aim to follow Christ's example by teaching "eternal truths through parables about people." It would stress "prophetic religion," emphasizing the Methodist view that personal holiness and concern for justice in the social order belonged together, and that the Christian's duty involved both. It would bring Methodism into the home and encourage every family member to grow in her or his faith by regular features for every age level.[5] Ongoing columns, such as "Together with the Small Fry," "Teens Together," and "Together in the Home," highlighted real-life families and how they solved their problems.

While looking at these concrete Methodist families, it is also helpful to follow the official resolutions and statements of the quadrennial General Conference, the only body that can speak for the (United) Methodist Church as a whole. Methodologically, one can get a more complete view of the Methodist family by looking at both official denominational stands and some examples of real Methodists living them out.

Together helped Methodists to define the ideal family. In "We Took a Tip from Susanna Wesley," readers were introduced to the DeGolier family of Brocton, New York. With two parents and twenty children (by birth!), this farming family only functioned because the older children were trained to care for the younger ones and each child had a regular schedule of household chores. The parents spent most of the day working in the fields and running their truck farm. The DeGoliers worked and played together and were actively involved in the Brocton Methodist Church. Two years later, the Detweilers of Burbank, California, were named the 1958 Methodist Family of the Year because, the judges said, "the Detweilers so well typify Methodist families the country over who put Christian ideas and ideals into their lives seven days each week."[6] The father, James, was a research engineer; his wife, Dorothy, was a homemaker. They and their three children, ages 17, 15, and 11, were all very involved in their local Methodist church. James was the church's lay leader, Dorothy was church school superintendent, the two teenagers were active in the Methodist Youth Fellowship, and the youngest child was an acolyte. Their pastor said of the Detweilers, "as individuals and as a family unit they are completely dedicated to Christ."[7] The family members were described as good neighbors as well as good Christians. Although there are significant differences between these two "ideal" Methodist families, they were both very traditional: breadwinner/homemaker, intact, and with children. They were also white and middle class. The Methodist Church had not yet begun to envision the family diversity that was soon to come.

Postwar Methodists, like those today, were deeply concerned about family stability and survival. The 1944 Discipline noted that the home was under attack and expressed concern about the increase in divorce and juvenile delinquency. It affirmed as the "birthright" of every child the emotional security of a stable home with two parents "living together and loving each other," and the religious security of a church-centered home. Among its recommendations were sex education for teenagers (ideally in the home, but if not, in the church), the instruction of youth in the Christian ideals of love, courtship, and marriage, and premarital counseling. "To save the child," it said, "you must save the home."[8]

The 1952 General Conference defined the Christian home as a place where parents practiced the presence of God, enabling their children to accept God as the greatest reality of life. It was assumed that to be a family meant to have children and to aim to bring every member into "the Christian way of life." There was mention of adoption, and the need to minister to those who had experienced "broken marriages," but the Methodist Church continued to urge that "divorce is not the answer."[9]

In 1956, the General Conference firmed up and expanded this definition of the Christian family and reaffirmed it in 1960. The Christian family was one in which parents lived the Christian life and each member was accepted and respected as a person of sacred worth. Again, as in 1952, the purpose of the Christian family was that all its members might come to accept God's love as the greatest reality in life and, in response, might grow spiritually, committed to Christian ideals of "personal conduct and social righteousness." This statement warned against "mixed marriages" (referring to persons of different religious backgrounds), affirmed planned parenthood "in Christian conscience," and urged that divorce was not the answer to marital difficulties—the church should try to help couples contemplating divorce to find other ways of overcoming their difficulties.[10] The traditional model was assumed, but many changes were at hand.

1960–1980:
"Being Transformed and Transforming"[11]

The 1960s and 1970s signaled great change for the United States, and also for Methodist families. This period is best understood as one of transition from the traditional norms of the past to something yet unknown. As the years progressed, every aspect of Methodist definition of Christian family was questioned and evaluated, using as the norm the Wesleyan quadrilateral of scripture, tradition, reason, and experience. Despite the questioning and rapid social change, Methodists maintained a vision of family as the basic unit of human community through which people came to know God's redemptive love. The content intended by God remained, but the form underwent major change.

The Reyes family of New Jersey appeared in the first issue of *Together* in 1960. Anastacio, his wife Josefina, and their two children sound like the ideal American Methodist family, displaying commitment to Jesus Christ seven days a week in church, work, and play. Anastacio had played professional baseball and had earned the Bronze and Silver Stars in World War II. Josefina used her skills as a seamstress to make the family's furniture slip covers and many of their clothes. Their son played ball with his dad, and their daughter was learning to sew and cook. The entire family was active in Bible studies and Sunday school at Lafayette Methodist Church, where Anastacio served as the church's lay leader.

Although ideal, they were not typical. During this period, most Methodists were white and either suburban or rural,[12] but the Reyes were Puerto Rican, having recently moved to Jersey City. They said they would like to move to the suburbs someday, but that they were happy in the city among Jersey City's 7,000 Puerto Rican immigrants. They were content to have the steady income from Anastacio's job at an electrical manufacturing firm in addition to Josefina's earnings from a garment factory. Their church involvement went beyond the typical study groups. The whole family was involved in the Methodist Center, an inner-city, multiethnic storefront church where worship was offered in Spanish as well as English.

The Reyes family illustrates the beginning of change for Methodist families. Although starting to embrace the diversity of the coming decades, they were also holding on to much that was dear. Methodists clearly heard the call to inner-city ministries. They were also finally willing to make attempts at racial inclusivity, as witnessed in the 1968 elimination of the Central Jurisdiction, a nongeographic segregation of black Methodists nationwide. That inclusivity stopped at mixed marriages though, both racial and religious, about which Methodists were warned until 1976. The first strong statement in support of diverse family forms appeared in the 1980 Discipline. But as early as 1960, Methodists were beginning to acknowledge racial diversity in church families. They were less prepared to face some of the other issues that affected the family, however, such as divorce, the women's movement, family planning, and numerous social issues associated with modernization.

The Methodist struggle with divorce came to a head in 1960. As early as 1884, the Methodist Episcopal Church had decided that remarriage after divorce should be limited only to those who were "innocent" parties in cases of adultery. Formal discussions, both for and against the rule, occurred throughout the Methodist Church after 1956, when a change was proposed. Despite the variety of positions, all agreed that, because of the spread of divorce, the institution of marriage was in danger and that the Methodist Church needed to provide strong programs to strengthen family unity.[13] The rule was liberalized in 1960, and the Methodist Church took its current position supporting marriage while allowing for divorce. In good Wesleyan fashion, Methodists were inclined to favor grace over precepts. Just one year later, in March 1961,

Together carried an article titled, "How to Treat Your Divorced Friends." A woman expressed her frustration at the lack of tact and kindness shown in response to her divorce. She hoped the Methodist Church would lead in teaching people how to be supportive of those recently divorced. Full acceptance would take years, but the stage had been set for significant changes.

Such changes can be measured by noting the state of the debate toward the end of this period. United Methodist laity had settled the topic of divorce for themselves, but not for their clergy. In April 1975, an article by the Rev. Dale White in *United Methodists Today* requested that clergy families be treated like all others in the church. He asserted that Protestants had long considered divorce to be a redemptive way to end a marriage that only distorted the intentions of God in the family. If redemptive for some United Methodists, it had to be available to all. White recognized the importance of the marriage commitment in the New Testament, but he also remembered Jesus' rebuke to his mother and brothers when they tried to claim the privilege of his family loyalty. Although the kin-based family is important, its value is only when it serves as agent to the kingdom of God through the greater community of the world. White stated, "Jesus would have been amazed at our idolatry of the incredibly shrunken, competitive, image-conscious, middle-class American family." Rather than focusing on divorce, he argued that Methodists needed to assess the insistence on an empty form of family without the Christian content of God's love.

Another issue involved the women's movement and specifically the role of the Methodist mother. Once again, *Together* is a helpful forum for assessing the variety of Methodist positions. Each issue carried a "Midmonth Powwow" in which Methodists expressed opinions, both pro and con, regarding topics raised in previous issues. The Powwow in January 1960 was titled, "The Women Agree to Disagree about Working Mothers." Four women supported working mothers, while five were opposed. Of the four who did support working mothers, two felt they "had to" work to make ends meet, and would rather have stayed home, doing "housework, baking, and taking care of the children." (It is likely that they all did these things in addition to an outside job anyway.) The other two, however, expressed frustration with the isolation of the home and the unending demands of housework and family. As is common, Methodists disagreed, but the majority still pictured motherhood as a fulfilling and full-time job for women.

Later that year, the July 1960 "Midmonth Powwow" asked, "Should

Marilyn Marry or Should She Go to College?" A promising young girl, described as having both "personality and ability," Marilyn was not planning to go to college because she wanted only to marry and raise a family. Her plans were addressed by a woman psychologist, a male seminary student, a university president, and a young woman who had recently graduated from college. All agreed that Marilyn should go to college, if only to prepare for marriage and children. Families, as well as society overall, demanded the most highly educated citizens possible. Marriage was not disparaged, but education was becoming a valuable asset for Methodist women. The recent graduate added that four years of college could provide important learning about men, so that she would be better able to select a husband. The psychologist stressed that she would also have a career to "fall back on." Education was essential, but marriage and motherhood were still the norm.

By 1965, the winds seemed to be blowing in the direction of working mothers. In a series titled, "People Called Methodists," the January 1965 issue of *Together* highlighted a "two-job family." This family of six left their house before dawn and did not return until late afternoon. Fred Jackson was an electrician and Joyce, a kindergarten teacher. The three oldest children went to school, and the baby stayed with Joyce's mother. Not only was the family busy at work and at home, but all family members were active in their Methodist church, where Fred chaired numerous committees and Joyce was the choir director. Significantly, the article praised the Jacksons for their ability to do everything, and to do it well. Joyce was described as a "housewife, mother, and schoolteacher," whereas Fred was portrayed as a "husband, father, community-church leader, and electrician." They were both expected to parent, provide leadership at church, and work in the community.

However, the controversy was not over. In May 1969, *Together* carried an article titled, "Should You Be a Working Mother?" The author stated that more harm was done to working mothers and their families by their numerous critics than by their work outside the home. Since the fact that many mothers worked was a given, the authors urged readers to examine the effects on the family so that potential damage could be avoided. Just one month later, in June 1969, another article titled "I'm Surviving Housewifery—I Think," extolled the virtues of the joyful housewife as one who designed her career to fit around her deeper commitment to family.

Although some United Methodists called themselves feminists and others traditionalists, none could ignore the challenges the women's movement posed for the family. After 1972, resolutions were consistently passed that called for the elimination of sex-role stereotyping in church and family. The women's movement was calling into question the previous definitions of motherhood, again requiring Methodists to reconsider the redemptive qualities of earlier family patterns and specifically women's role in them.

The size of the DeGolier family, earlier heralded as a model for Methodists, was both valued and increasingly viewed as problematic as Methodists recognized concerns about overpopulation. Until 1960, family planning was important because it allowed couples to have only the children they truly wanted. The 1964 Discipline added the larger social concern about "population explosion." In January 1965, *Together* reflected this change of focus, carrying an article on overpopulation and the religious obligation to limit family size. Americans were praised for success in controlling the birthrate so far, citing 75 percent of Protestant couples deliberately limiting their reproduction. Methodists were assumed to be already concerned and aware, and they were encouraged to educate others on the basis of their ethical commitments. On the other hand, the 1972 General Conference, at the end of the resolution on infertility, cited overpopulation as a "distinct problem which should not be subsumed in a general statement about parenthood or the environment." Couples unable to have children due to infertility problems were the focus of the statement, whereas limiting family size seemed an afterthought. Also, the focus was on "world overpopulation" as a global topic and not specifically an issue for American United Methodist families. As with most issues, Methodists were found holding every position, and using theological analysis to undergird their views.

Social change was occurring both within the family and around it, and both were of interest to United Methodists because their theology had always addressed both private and social holiness. The spring 1976 unit of *Christian Studies,* the United Methodist Sunday School materials for young elementary school students, focused on the theme of change. In one session, the students were asked to study a picture of a father in an apron, bringing dinner to the table while the mother watched television with the children. They were asked to describe the change and the difference it might make for them. The publishers evidently were aware of family changes and wanted to help children understand from a Christian perspective that God's love could be expressed in the new forms.

United Methodists were also called to spread the love from their families to their communities by taking stands on social issues. That year's summer unit of the same Sunday school materials highlighted the Gonzales family, who were being asked to sign a petition against open housing in their neighborhood for people of all races. At their family meeting, they decided that it would be against their Christian principles to sign, and that they were willing to accept the negative reactions from their neighbors for their refusal. Victor Gonzales, the young son, concluded by saying, "We just cannot sign that paper. We are a Christian family. Christians show they are Christians by their love for everyone."[14] The United Methodist Church wanted their families to take social stands as families, in that families were to be a witness to God's love.

Together, in trying to present the diversity of Methodist opinions, was often ahead of the thinking of the General Church. Although Methodists shared this basic commitment to social justice, the content of their opinions varied along the entire spectrum. Partially as a result of falling subscriptions because of reader protests, *Together* ceased publication in 1973.[15] The Methodist magazine for families seemed to disappear just as the Methodist understanding of family was being redefined. At the start of this period, in 1960, the definition of the "Christian family" assumed the inclusion of parents (plural) and children. The presence of grandparents was also acknowledged. In 1968, the definition of family was refined to include those related by marriage, birth, or adoption. By 1980, a number of new forms were affirmed, including foster parents, single parents, couples without children, and even friends sharing the same residence, or families of choice.

At the end of these decades, the family magazine was gone, along with the ability to depict a "typical" United Methodist family, but statements and resolutions on the family remained strong, visionary, and replete with recommendations for action to eliminate family violence, protect children's rights, and discern moral values. United Methodist ministry always included the protection, nurturance, and strengthening of the family. United Methodists continued to experience and avow the importance of family as the expression of God's love in intimate human relationships, even as their emphasis on grace persuaded them to be open to the many forms it might take. The next period would challenge them even more.

1980–1995:
" 'Real Life' Family Values"[16]

The November–December 1995 issue of a current United Methodist magazine, *Interpreter,* related the story of the multiracial and multigenerational Hard family of Buffalo, New York. Barbara Hard is the single mother of two young girls she adopted from Russia and a teenage foster son from Vietnam. Her seventy-seven-year-old mother also lives with them. Although uncomfortable when she had six Vietnamese foster children, the church finds it easier to accept the Russian girls because they are white. Although still working through its prejudices, Barbara says that the church has always tried to be supportive of her family. In the same issue of *Interpreter,* Marilyn McGee, director of United Methodist Family Ministries, states that compassion and acceptance must be at the center of the United Methodist Church's outreach to families. Family values have been defined too narrowly by politicians and others who believe that only traditional families deserve the church's support. She asks that United Methodists discard family myths and welcome all people, being sensitive to the variety of family and household models and encouraging all types of families to see themselves as whole.

This may be the vision of the future more than the reality of today, although some issues have garnered consensus. Divorce, for example, is no longer as controversial as it was in the past. The United Methodist Church now seeks to minister to divorced persons by addressing their pain as well as the potential for personal growth. The new 1992 version of the *Book of Worship* includes a service for healing of persons going through divorce, which specifically cites the "acceptance of new realities." This has been one of the themes of the turbulent period since the 1960s and 1970s, during which United Methodists have continued to struggle with new family issues.

The ordination of women has presented new issues that may not have been anticipated when women were first given full clergy rights in 1956. This has been especially prominent in the United Methodist Church because of the itinerant system that includes guaranteed appointment for all clergy, regardless of sex. Combined with the large size of the denomination, that means there are more clergywomen in the United Methodist Church than in any other denomination. The itinerant process of moving pastors at the discretion of bishops and their cabinets has become a challenge. Earlier, the church expected male clergy

to marry, raise families, and move frequently. Husbands had little problem uprooting their families, who understood that this was the norm
for the Methodist parsonage family. Married women clergy, however,
have been less willing to ask husbands to move away from lucrative jobs
and professional commitments. In addition, the modern wives of clergymen have begun to value their own careers, also requesting longer
tenures. As a result, clergy in general have been less willing to relocate
regularly, wanting instead to settle for longer periods to nurture both
the churches and their families.

Clergy couples have added another challenge. Many of these couples
share all of the tasks of church and home. When one clergyman was
asked where he and his clergy wife lived, he said it depended on who
was cooking supper that night. A clergywoman who was asked about
her husband's church responded by saying that she didn't know about
it because she didn't attend there.[17] These responses indicate some of
the confusion over the role of the clergyperson and the role of the
spouse. While these clergymen may also have household responsibilities, clergywomen may not fulfill the expectations of the traditional
clergy wife. In spite of this, most congregations are excited about the
ministry of clergy couples and the new ways they approach the challenges of church and home. They exemplify a new form of shared responsibility—a model for many United Methodists who wish to share
home and family obligations.

The inclusive nature of the United Methodist Church is now being
expressed and honored in the growing numbers of interethnic and interracial couples. Mel Williams, an African-American minister, and his
wife Virginia, a Filipino-American deaconess, witness to the grace that
can be manifest in the church. His acceptance as pastor in a United
Methodist church in Manila, as well as the love she receives in black
churches where they work together, testify to the United Methodist
Church's ability to break down barriers that separate people in secular
society. Although the United Methodist Church is still "going on to per-
fection" (the goal of all United Methodists) in this and many areas, the
fact that the Williamses were honored in the November 1980 *New
World Outlook,* an official publication of the church, shows that racism
is no longer acceptable in the United Methodist Church. The warnings
about mixed marriages in the 1950s have become celebrations of love
in diversity.

The most recent challenge to the United Methodist Church's understanding of family has come around the question of the acceptance of

homosexuality. Since 1972, the United Methodist position, as expressed in the Social Principles, has been that the practice of homosexuality is "incompatible with Christian teaching." Although this is clearly the official position, the issue has been raised and put to a vote at every General Conference. In 1992, about 75 percent of the body supported maintaining this position, which indicates both the majority opinion and also the existence of a significant minority.

Homosexual families are still not accepted in most United Methodist Churches, but signs of change are unmistakable. Bishop Melvin E. Wheatley once said, "Homosexuality is a mysterious gift of God's grace."[18] The national gay, lesbian, and bisexual caucus of the United Methodist Church, Affirmation, endorses this position and, in 1984, started the Reconciling Congregations program. Churches that pursue "Reconciling" status vote to affirm and advertise their acceptance of all people, regardless of sexual orientation. By the end of 1995, there were ninety-one Reconciling Congregations. In response, the Evangelical Renewal Fellowship of the California-Nevada Conference launched the Transforming Congregations program to provide healing and integration into the local church for repentant homosexuals. As of the same date, there were thirty-eight Transforming Congregations.

Jeanne Knepper, a United Methodist clergywoman, feels a double call: to ministry and to family life with her partner and their two daughters.[19] If and when homosexual people are accepted fully into the United Methodist Church, new forms of family will become acceptable as well. But as always, while the forms may change, the content remains the same: The family is the place where God's love is manifest and taught, and where each person is valued as a child of God. Tex Sample, professor at one of the United Methodist seminaries, believes that full acceptance of gays and lesbians is just a matter of time.[20] If history is any indication, he is correct, because among United Methodists, grace has been an important guiding principle for action.

Conclusion:
"Acceptance, Compassion . . . and a
Different Set of Rules"[21]

Because United Methodists are now divided on how to define the family, it has become difficult to speak out strongly on its behalf. The 1984 *Book of Resolutions* was the last to make a statement specifically on the family. The resolution of 1988 addresses policies for families with children only. The other family-related concerns are addressed under each specific issue, such as divorce, domestic violence, or sexuality. Strong support of families is still asserted in the Social Principles, but the lack of recent resolutions on family may be indicative of the current disagreement as to the form families take.

Many believe that Christian churches have been slow to respond to the changing needs of newer forms. The typical United Methodist family is now, much like the typical American family, likely to include single parents with children, blended families, adults caring for aging parents, foster parents, and so on. It has become much harder to address the plethora of needs. However, the official documents, the personal lives of United Methodists, and church programs—childcare centers, food pantries, step-family or divorce support groups—indicate that much has been happening.

Although the popular press may bemoan the lack of morals and family values in society in general, strong moral convictions do not seem to be missing among active United Methodists. Deliberations in the General Church will continue to struggle with the changing forms but, at the grassroots level, United Methodist people have already begun living the changes and adjusting as necessary. Overall, the Methodist emphasis on grace means that acceptance and compassion must be the norms. Koyla Braun, family issues specialist with the Board of Global Ministries, recently called United Methodists to a more biblical notion of family in which everyone is a brother or sister and the family is the family of God.[22] Perhaps this is the future. Historically, Methodists have consciously tried to fashion their values by faith rather than by cultural standards. Once again, United Methodists may have to move away from those in politics and popular culture who define family too narrowly. In so doing, they will embody Wesley's teaching that God's grace is available to all.

NOTES

'Tis Grace Will Lead Us Home is taken from John Newton, "Amazing Grace," in *The United Methodist Hymnal: Book of United Methodist Worship*, (Nashville: The United Methodist Publishing House, 1989), 378.

1. John Wesley, "A Plain Account of Genuine Christianity," in *John Wesley*, ed. Albert C. Outler (New York: Oxford University Press, 1964), 184.
2. In 1968, the Methodist Church merged with the Evangelical United

Brethren to become the United Methodist Church. Both "Methodist" and "United Methodist" will be used here as appropriate to the period.

3. Gregory Schneider, "Social Religion, the Christian Home, and Republican Spirituality in Antebellum Methodism," in *Perspectives on American Methodism: Interpretive Essays,* ed. Russell E. Richey, Kenneth E. Rowe, and Jean Miller Schmidt (Nashville: Kingswood Books, Abingdon Press, 1993), 200, 205–6.

4. *Together* 1:1 (October 1956): 22.

5. Lovick Pierce and J. Edgar Washabaugh, "Statement from the Publishing Agents," *Together* 1:1 (October 1956): 9.

6. "Meet: Methodist Family of the Year," *Together* 2:11 (November 1958): 14.

7. Ibid., 15.

8. *Doctrines and Discipline of The Methodist Church 1944* (Nashville: The Methodist Publishing House in association with Whitmore & Stone, 1944), 559–60.

9. *Doctrines and Discipline of The Methodist Church 1952* (Nashville: The Methodist Publishing House in association with Pierce and Washabaugh, 1952), 636, 638.

10. *Doctrines and Discipline of The Methodist Church 1956* (Nashville: The Board of Publications of The Methodist Church, Inc., 1957), 708–10.

11. *The Book of Resolutions of the United Methodist Church 1984,* (Nashville: The United Methodist Publishing House, 1984), 290.

12. Leo Roston, ed., *Religions of America: Ferment and Faith in an Age of Crisis* (New York: Simon & Schuster, 1975), 451.

13. Finis A. Crutchfield, "Should Methodism Liberalize Its Rules on Marrying Divorced Persons?" *Together* 4:4 (April 1960): 28.

14. *Christian Studies,* Vacation Bible School 1:4 (Summer 1976): sec. 2.

15. Willis J. Heydenberk, "The *Together* 'Bold Venture': A Methodist Magazine, 1956–1973," (M.A. Thesis, University of Missouri-Columbia, 1977), 112.

16. Paige McKenzie, " 'Real Life' Family Values," *Interpreter* 39:8 (November–December 1995): 14.

17. Martha A. Lane, "When Ministers Are Married—To Each Other!" *United Methodists Today* 1:2 (February 1974): 19.

18. James V. Heidinger II, "25 Years of Vision," *Good News* (March/April 1992):17.

19. Jeanne Knepper, "Turning Walls into Arches: A Metaphor for Change in the Church," *Open Hands* 10:3 (Winter 1995):18.

20. Tex Sample, quoted in "Social Principles Upheld," *Good News* (May/June 1992): 12.

21. McKenzie, "Real Life," 14–17.

22. Ibid., 15.

7

American Jewry: Families of Tradition in American Culture

SYLVIA BARACK FISHMAN

Patterns in Jewish family life in America, while reflecting developing ideas from within the community, have also been profoundly affected by larger historical and sociological trends and by the interaction between Judaic lifestyles and ideas, as well as those prevalent in the larger cultural environment.[1] Therefore, current debates over the history and fate of the American family, and the struggle between the values of individualism and those of familism and communalism, have special significance for the American Jewish community.[2]

The Jewish household has undergone a gradual metamorphosis, moving more and more into conformity with the family units of middle- and upper-middle-class white, well-educated Christians. The traditional familism of the Jewish community has, over the years, been transformed by American individualist ideals. Nevertheless, there are interesting areas in which the Jewish community differs from non-Jewish families and within itself along denominational lines.

The post–World War II American cultural emphasis on marriage and the family reinforced Jewish values that had been in place for hundreds of years. Traditionally, the Jewish emphasis on marriage begins at birth. The male child, when he is ritually circumcised, and the female child, when she is named in the synagogue, each receive a blessing, asking that they will mature into marriage and good deeds and (for boys) the study of Torah. That blessing is repeated at each official milestone in the child's life, for Judaism views marriage not as a necessary compromise to human frailties but as the most productive state for adult human beings. Informally as well, the emphasis on marriage permeates language, attitudes, and behavior.

Within traditional Jewish culture, marriage was seen as the only salutary and productive state for adult human beings. There were few comfortable cultural niches for an adult without spouse and children. There were no celibate clergy and there was no tradition of a son or daughter remaining unmarried to care for a widowed father or mother. Jewish congregations tended to avoid hiring an unmarried rabbi or religious teacher, and a child who remained unwed often was regarded by parents as a source of shame. In a similar way, it was unheard of for a Jewish couple deliberately to remain childless.

Partially as a result of this overwhelming cultural bias, Jewish men and women in the United States have, until recently, almost universally achieved marriage (over 95 percent) by the time they were well into their reproductive years. Analyses based on the 1970 National Jewish Population Study (NJPS), for example, show that in 1970, 95 percent of American Jewish females were married by age 34; 96 percent of American Jewish males, by age 39. Although Jews married one to three years later, on average, than other whites in the United States, more of them ended up married.[3] Although until recently American Jews have long had smaller families than other ethnic groups, they cherished children. During the past two-and-a-half decades, however, the social climate of the United States has undergone dramatic changes and, for Jews as for all Americans, family configurations have become increasingly diverse.

Data from the 1990 NJPS provide today's social scientists with information about Jews in the United States. When these national data are used in combination with studies conducted by almost two dozen individual Jewish communities, they reveal a picture of sweeping national change and individual geographic variations. For example, comparisons between 1970 and today show that marriage rates have declined sharply in the American Jewish community to the point where it resembles the non-Jewish community far more than the American Jewish community of 1970. About two-thirds of today's Jews are married, compared to nearly four-fifths of Jews in 1970. As the 1990s began, fewer than two-thirds of all Americans were married, more than one-fifth had never been married, 7 percent of Jews and 8 percent of all Americans were widowed, and 8 percent of both groups were currently divorced.

For American Jews, as for other Americans today, there is no one model of the family.[4] Jewish households in the United States include the traditional, two-parent family with clearly differentiated masculine and feminine roles; the ultra-Orthodox two-parent family with many children; the dual-career, two-parent family; singles and divorced households without children; single-parent families; and elderly couples of widowed "singles." The number of Orthodox Jews has declined only slightly since the 1970s whereas the number of Conservative Jews has declined substantially. However, the proportion identifying themselves as Reform has grown. The greatest increase is seen in the proportion of Jews who call themselves "just Jewish" (Jewish but not by religion), or secular or cultural Jews.

As might be expected, the most traditional Jewish family patterns are found today among Orthodox Jews, whose lifestyles in general are the most conservative along the spectrum of American Jewish life. They are the only cohort among contemporary American Jews for whom the normative age of marriage for both males and females falls in the eighteen to twenty-four age group. They have the fewest number of childless women, the highest rate of actual fertility, and the highest rate of expected fertility among women aged eighteen to forty-four. Orthodox rates of mixed marriage are about one-third of those of the rest of the population. While there are many ideological differences between Conservative and Reform American Jews, they are basically similar in terms of family formation.

Dual-Career Families

Among Jewish couples in every denomination, dual-career families are the norm. The significant number of contemporary Jewish women seeking higher levels of education translates into shifting occupational profiles. The vast majority of Jewish women in college today assume they will be labor-force participants for most of their lives. They plan for that labor-force participation and educate themselves for it; the days when college functioned as a kind of intellectual finishing school, or exclusively as a preparation for intelligent motherhood, seem to be past. Moreover, Jewish college women not only take for granted that they will work, they often assume that they have the right to choose self-fulfilling and financially rewarding work.

The labor force participation of Jewish women today departs radically from patterns of the recent past. Feminism and other social and economic factors have ensured that American Jewish women are much more likely to be paid employees than were American Jewish women at mid-century. The majority continue to work outside the home throughout their childbearing and childrearing years. The NJPS indicated that among American Jewish women aged forty-four and under, 70 percent work for pay (59 percent work full time and 11 percent work part time), only 17 percent are homemakers, 11 percent are students, and 4 percent are not employed. In this survey, numbers were rounded up to the next highest whole number, and thus may add up to more than 100 percent.

Despite the demographic change represented by these patterns, studies have shown that women who are firmly grounded in Jewish life can enjoy success both in wife-mother roles and in career roles.[5] Compromise and mutual support are keys to a successful working relationship. Although family life may often be less than perfect, if both spouses are firmly committed to their relationship and to their children, they will roll with the punches, and will usually emerge with arrangements that are satisfactory for them both. In a study of nearly 500 married, dual-career couples, researchers discovered that the character of the husband is the key to a successful dual-career marriage.[6]

Studies have also shown that working Jewish women are often committed to their religion. A Washington, D.C., area study of ninety-seven Jewish career women with three or more children found that eighty-six women were members of Reform, Conservative, or Orthodox synagogues, three belonged to havurot, two were Reconstructionists, and only six had no religious affiliation.[7] Over half the women invited to participate in the survey "said that Jewish beliefs and attitudes helped them to juggle their multiple obligations. . . . Several stated that religion and tradition 'held them together'" as the family worked through crisis situations. One-third of the respondents kept kosher homes, more than half had some form of Sabbath observance, and three-quarters sent their children to religious school—with one-fifth in day schools. It is significant that among these working women strong religious identification was not a factor of being closer to the immigrant generation: religious observance was more pronounced among younger than older respondents.[8]

Intermarriage

A shrinking Jewish population in America, due to the twin forces of intermarriage and assimilation, constitutes a major cause of concern today, as does the religious identity of children raised in Jewish homes. In the United States, intermarriage between Jews and non-Jews began to rise in the mid-1960s, rose sharply thereafter, continued to climb in the 1980s, and is now commonplace. As a result, in many Jewish communities today, "out" marriages outnumber "in" marriages. This change in the underlying social and religious structure of the American Jewish community has important implications for the future. Marriage to non-Jews has increased partially because of the successful integration of Jews into American society and partially because of their achieving a high level of social acceptance. However, intermarriage may reflect and contribute to the decline of Judaism in America.

The subject of intermarriage evokes considerable passion among Jews because it arouses elemental fears of group survival. One aspect of the matter is quantitative: The offspring of intermarriage may not remain Jewish, so within one or two generations there may be fewer Jews and a greatly weakened Jewish community. Another aspect is qualitative: Even if intermarriage does not lead to a decrease in the physical number of persons living in households with a Jewish parent, questions remain as to their Jewishness—that is, the intensity of their communal affiliation, ethnic identification, and religious practice.[9]

Intensive Jewish education is clearly associated with a reduced likelihood of marrying outside the faith. Those receiving more than six years of either supplementary school education or day school education are much less likely to marry a non-Jew than those receiving more minimal forms of Jewish education. Jewish day school education reduces the likelihood of a mixed marriage no matter in which branch of Judaism the person had been raised. The clear association between Jewish education and marrying within the faith is strongest among younger American Jews. Overall, about one-fifth of Jews aged twenty-five to forty-four who had received six or more years of day school education married non-Jews compared to half of those who had received six or more years of supplementary school, and three-fifths of Jews who had received some supplementary school or Sunday school, and two-thirds of those who received no Jewish education.[10] In addition, those Jews who received an extensive Jewish education were much more likely to have spouses who converted to Judaism than those who did not.[11]

Children of mixed marriages have their core identities formed in competing heritages. Thus a mixed marriage not only decreases the likelihood that an unambiguous Jewish identity will be formed, but also raises the possibility that no Jewish identity at all will emerge. As Nathan Glazer has explained, "Their children have alternatives before them that the children of families in which both parents were born Jewish do not—they have legitimate alternative identities."[12] They can incorporate the identity of the Jewish parent, that of the non-Jewish parent, that of both, or that of neither. Identifying wholly with one parent may prove traumatic to the extent that it involves the rejection of the other parent, and it can trigger self-rejection as well. Maintaining both identities simultaneously may create tensions and conflicts. The most commonly chosen solution is to identify with neither parent religiously and to focus instead on shared, general, secular values.

The Singles

During the 1970s, the singles' state, for the first time in Jewish history, became an extended period in the adult life cycle rather than a short way-station between childhood and adulthood. For more than a decade, the singles' culture was celebrated by the media as an exhilarating, vital way of life. Like others in their socioeconomic class, Jewish men born in the late 1940s and the 1950s seemed uninterested in early commitments; when they did marry, they usually chose younger women, rather than choosing someone from their age group. In addition, many more Jewish men than women intermarried, leaving a sizeable proportion of Jewish women unmarried.[13]

A growing emphasis on feminist aspiration and achievement also contributed to later marriage and childbearing. Jewish women were prominent among the roster of militant feminists who exhorted women not to be lured into the twin slaveries of marriage and motherhood. Rather than viewing job skills as useful for earning money in cases of necessity, women sought professional careers in much the same way as men. Jewish women, who had had comparatively high educational levels, excelled in this new atmosphere of expanding opportunities, and they often postponed marriage and a family.

By the 1980s, however, large numbers of unmarried Jews were openly searching for ways to combine the pleasures of achievement with the more traditional and companionable joys of family life and community participation. Singles and community leaders alike sought ways of encouraging single Jews to interact more within the Jewish community. Jewish dating services, both commercial and not-for-profit, have proliferated in major metropolitan areas. Some modern versions of the traditional *shadchan* (matchmaker) utilize "computer matching" of eligible men and women. Some rely exclusively on the interview process to match and bring together likely prospects; others combine both methods.[14]

Homosexual households are newly visible in the Jewish community.

Gay and lesbian congregations exist in such cities as Baltimore, Cambridge, Cleveland, Dallas, Miami, Minneapolis, Montreal, Philadelphia, New York, San Francisco, Seattle, Washington, D.C., as well as elsewhere in North America.[15] In addition, most major college campuses have Jewish gay and lesbian societies. Precise figures on the proportion of homosexuals in the Jewish community—as in the general American community—are difficult to obtain. Estimates as to the percentages of homosexuals in given communities have varied widely and are the subject of considerable disagreement. A proliferating number of books and articles on the subject of Jewish homosexuality indicate that the Jewish homosexual community includes many who remain deeply involved in Jewish life.

Divorced Jews

The divorce rate among Jews, as among other Americans, increased significantly in the 1970s and 1980s. Some contemporary divorces may be linked to the changing role of women in today's society. Men and women experiencing marital difficulties today often are less committed to the permanence of marriage and prefer to begin a new life rather than to work out the problems of the old. Popular culture also subverts the efforts of couples struggling to deal with marital conflict. The media often presents compromise as antithetical to personal integrity and self-esteem. The idea that parents should make sacrifices in order to maintain the family unit is often seen as outmoded. Judith Wallerstein recalls Margaret Mead's troubled reflections on the rising rate of divorce: "There is no society in the world where people have stayed married without enormous community pressure to do so."[16]

Given the educational and economic skills to be self-supporting, women are far less likely than in the past to remain in an unhappy marriage. In addition, some men who expected a submissive wife are outraged when their spouses grow into different roles. Orthodox Jewish feminist, and mother of five, Blu Greenberg insists

> it goes without saying that feminism has had a powerful impact on the rising divorce rate in the Jewish community. As a young, divorced rabbi recently put it when asked why he divorced: "My ex-wife got into this women's liberation thing, and I was too immature to know how to cope with it." (He was being kind in not saying that his wife also did not know how to cope with it.) I am convinced that three-fourths of the marriages that succeed could

have come apart at ten different points along the way, and some three-fourths of the marriages that fail could have been put back together again at twenty points along the way. A great deal has to do with how one negotiates the inevitable impasses in an intimate relationship.[17]

All denominations of Jewry have been influenced by the American propensity to divorce, but religious observance still has an inverse relationship to the number of divorces. Jay Brodbar-Nemzer found that Jews with a low rate of ritual observance are eight times more likely to be divorced at some point in their lives than are Jews who have a greater commitment to traditional Jewish observance.[18] However, it is not uncommon today for marriages even among the ultra-Orthodox to be in trouble, and the Orthodox Rabbinical Court (*Bet Din*) of New York reports that divorce rates are rising among Orthodox Jews and even among members of Hasidic sects.[19] Perhaps the socialization gap is partially responsible. Young Orthodox women have some acquaintance with secular culture, but young Orthodox men are expected to focus exclusively on the study of sacred literature, often leaving social graces to chance.

Single-Parent Jewish Families

The number of Jewish single-parent families, like the number of divorces, seems insignificant at first glance; but this impression is deceptive. Single-parent families represent a relatively small percentage of the number of Jewish *households* in each city but, because of the generally low Jewish birthrate, the numbers become more significant when you factor in the number of *households with children*. Nationwide, an estimated one-third of Jewish children live in homes that have been touched by divorce, with approximately 10 percent living in single-parent homes and approximately 20 percent living in homes in which at least one parent has been previously divorced. These families have some unique problems. Jewish life cycle celebrations can pull these children in two directions. Children of single-parent families sometimes have difficulty dealing with the Jewish emphasis on family, particularly around holiday times. In response, some Jewish institutions have begun support programs to help broken families arrange life cycle celebrations with a minimum of trauma.

In the majority of cases, for Jews as well as non-Jews, the single-parent household is headed by a woman. Social and emotional factors, as well as financial factors, complicate life for the Jewish single-parent mother.[20] In a sense, the Jewish emphasis on family works against those whose families are no longer intact by making it difficult for them to find a niche in the community, thus making them feel even more isolated. When Jewish single parents reach out to the Jewish community, they may have difficulty finding a supportive peer group. The call for responsiveness from the Jewish community is legion among single parents.[21]

Childbearing: The Contemporary Jewish Family and Fertility

Concerned with the disturbing changes in Jewish family life in their area, Jewish communities across the country have compiled figures on the average number of children per family and the configuration of Jewish households. Data from the 1990 NJPS show that women who identify themselves as "Jewish by religion" are much more likely to have children than women who consider themselves to be secular Jews. Orthodox Jewish women are more likely to be married and have children and, as a group, Orthodox women alone are currently having children above replacement levels (2.1 children per family). Conservative women expect to have more children than Reform women, but few differences in actual family size exist among thirty-five- to forty-four-year-old Conservative and Reform women.[22]

The vast majority of Jewish women still place an enormous value on having children. They are less likely than any other religious or ethnic group to state that they wish to remain childless.[23] Most American Jewish couples hope to have children "some day." Unlike women of other ethnic groups, where higher education is associated with lower expectations of childbearing, the more highly educated a Jewish woman is, the more children she expects to have. Sociologists Calvin Goldscheider and Frances Kobrin Goldscheider, relying on data that deals with expected family size, point out that among Jewish populations—unlike among Protestants and Catholics—"educational attainment is directly rather than inversely related to the fertility expectations."[24]

Contrary to the expectations of both women and demographers, "as education increases among both Jewish men and women, the proportion with no children increases." Indeed, "among those with a master's degree . . . Jews have significantly higher levels of childlessness than non-Jews."[25] Among highly educated Jewish women today, expectations have dropped. Although Jewish career women are more committed to having families than any other group of career women, they are at least as likely as other white middle-class women to postpone the onset of childbearing until they have reached what they consider to be an appropriate level of financial or occupational achievement. Childlessness often is unintentional, however. When a couple conscientiously uses birth control as part of family planning, they do not imagine that promoting conception rather than preventing it one day will prove to be problematic.[26]

Conclusion

No aspect of contemporary American life has aroused as much anxiety and debate in the Jewish community as changes in family formation. Many American Jews feel caught between two value systems: an individualist American ethos that gives priority to an individual's talents, strengths, and opportunities, and a Jewish tradition that gives priority to the needs of the family unit and the community. The transformed Jewish family—like the transformed American family—has been influenced not only by feminism but by (1) widespread cultural attitudes that stress individual achievement and pleasure; (2) materialist expectations that elevate the perceived standard of what a "middle-class" lifestyle comprises; (3) a tightening economic market requiring dual incomes to maintain middle-class lifestyles; (4) the easy availability of contraceptive techniques and the accompanying sexual revolution; and (5) patterns of chronological separation that split families by sending adolescents to far-off university campuses and grandparents to the sunbelt.

The impact of changes in educational and occupational patterns on the American Jewish family appears to be ongoing. Singles probably will maintain an important presence among Jewish families as young adults pursue career goals and self-development in their twenties and thirties. In addition, it appears unlikely that American Jewish women will abandon educational and career opportunities; they probably will continue to marry later and bear their children later than earlier generations. As Jewish women retain career commitments even during their childbearing years, the dual-career family may become even more normative.

The changed lifestyles of American Jewish men and women today have had a powerful, and probably permanent, impact on the character of the American Jewish family. Jewish families today face the challenge of retaining their vitality and cohesion while responding to the opportunities of an open society. The responses of Jewish individuals, family units, and communal groups to these challenges has often been profoundly influenced by the denominational society in which they establish their Jewish religious and social lives.

Jewish households that define themselves as Orthodox and traditionalist Conservative usually retain more elements of Jewish family life common in some earlier, more Jewishly cohesive periods of Jewish history. They often utilize coping mechanisms such as compartmentalization—dividing their nonsectarian work lives from their Jewishly intensive home lives. Some traditionalists also engage in behaviors that reseal boundaries whose sweeping permeability seem to threaten their sense of Jewish distinctiveness. In contrast, among Americanized Conservative, Reform, and Reconstructionist Jews, the primary coping mechanism has been a kind of conflation of Jewish and American/Protestant values and behaviors, refashioned as "American Judaism." This bringing together of American and Jewish values and lifestyles has been enhanced by the presence of increasing numbers of non-Jews in Jewish households, especially in Americanized Jewish households.

At the present time, Americanized—rather than traditionalist— Jewish households are numerically prominent in American Jewish communities. However, among the leadership of the American Jewish community, traditionalist Jewish families are gaining prominence. This is true even of leadership in Jewish communal settings that were previously thought of as secular, such as Jewish federations, communal service organizations, and community relations organizations. The goals and attitudes of Jewish leaders, even those who function in nonreligious capacities and settings, have many commonalities with those of Jewish traditionalist laypersons. Only time will tell whether large groups of families that choose to remain within the purview of American Jewish communal life will, in the future, be more likely to resemble the behavior of today's traditionalists, or of coalescing, Americanized models.

NOTES

1. This chapter is based on data from the 1990 National Jewish Population Survey (NJPS) and recent studies of Jewish populations in individual communities. It includes materials presented in different form in two earlier

works: "The Changing American Jewish Family Faces the 1990s," in *The Jewish and Jewish Community,* ed. Steven Bayme and Gladys Rose (New York: Kta Publishing and the American Jewish Committee, 1994); and "The Changing American Jewish Family in the 80s," *Contemporary Jewry* 9 (1988): 1–33. These materials will later be included in a larger interpretive framework in Sylvia B. Fishman, *Changing Lifestyles of American Jewish Women and Men* (New York: SUNY Press, forthcoming). Special thanks are due my colleagues at the Maurice and Marilyn Cohen Center for Modern Jewish Studies at Brandeis University, especially: the late Marshall Sklare who introduced me to the sociological study of the Jews; Gary Tobin and Lawrence Sternberg for their ongoing support for and interest in my work on the Jewish family; research assistants Gabrielle Garschnia and Miriam Hertz for their competent performance of a variety of tasks, and Sylvia Riese, executive secretary, who was of invaluable assistance in expediting the revisions of this chapter. National statistics on the Jewish community in the United States are drawn from the 1990 NJPS conducted under the auspices of the Council of Jewish Federations. A summary of findings is provided by Barry Kosmin et al., *Highlights of the CJF 1990 National Jewish Population Survey* (New York: Council of Jewish Federations, 1991). Percentages in this chapter have been rounded from .5 to the next highest number.

2. Paula E. Hyman, "Introduction," in *The Jewish Family: Myths and Realities,* ed. Steven M. Cohen and Paula Hyman (New York: Holmes and Meier, 1986), 3–4. See also, Sylvia Barack Fishman, "Challenge for Jewish Educators: Children of the Fragmented Family," *Ideas on Jewish Education* (June 1983): 1–8.

3. U. O. Schmelz and S. DellaPergola, "The Demographic Consequences of U.S. Population Trends," *American Jewish Yearbook* (1983): 148–49.

4. Peggy Wireman, *Urban Neighborhoods, Networks, and Families: New Forms of Old Values* (Lexington, Mass.: Lexington Books, D.C. Heath Company, 1984), 6.

5. See, for example, Aileen Cohen Nusbacher, "The Orthodox Jewish Professional Woman" (M.A. Thesis in the Department of Sociology, Brooklyn College, January 1977); and Linda Gordon Kuzmack and George Salomon, *Working and Mothering: A Study of 97 Jewish Career Women with Three or More Children* (The National Jewish Family Center of the American Jewish Committee, 1980).

6. Dana Vannoy-Hiller and William W. Philliber, *Equal Partners: Successful Women in Marriage,* Sage Library of Social Research 174 (Newbury Park, Calif.: Sage Publications, 1989), 120–22.

7. Kuzmack and Salomon, *Working and Mothering,* 18.

8. Ibid., 23.

9. Peter Y. Medding et al., "Jewish Identity in Conversionary and Mixed Marriages," *American Jewish Year Book 1992* (New York: American Jewish Committee and Jewish Publication Society, 1992).

10. Sylvia Barack Fishman and Alice Goldstein, *When They are Grown They Will Not Depart: Jewish Education and the Jewish Behavior of American Adults,* a joint publication of the Cohen Center for Modern Jewish Studies, Council of Jewish Federations, and the Jewish Educational Service of North America (Waltham, Mass.: Brandeis University CMJS Research Report, 1993).

11. Robert N. Bellah, "Competing Visions of the Role of Religion in American Society," in *Uncivil Religion: Interreligious Hostility in America,* ed. Robert N. Bellah and Frederick E. Greenspahn (New York, Crossroad, 1987), 228.

12. Nathan Glazer, *New Perspectives in American Jewish Sociology* (New York: American Jewish Committee, 1987), 13.

13. William Novack, "Are Good Jewish Men a Vanishing Breed?" *Moment* 5 (January/February 1980): 14–20.

14. Among numerous newspaper articles and advertisements for Jewish dating services, see B. Drummond Ayres, Jr., "For Jewish Only, a Computer Dating Service," *The New York Times,* 27 June 1974; Judith L. Kuper, "2000 Singles Enrolled in Dating Service," *The Jewish Post and Opinion,* 16 July 1976; and Yitta Halberstam, "Today's Shadchan: Popular and Expensive," *Jewish Week,* 31 July 1977.

15. Jewish Telegraphic Agency, *Community News Reporter,* 11 April 1986.

16. Judith S. Wallerstein and Sandra Blakeslee, *Second Chances: Men, Women and Children a Decade after Divorce—Who Wins, Who Loses, and Why* (New York: Ticknor & Fields, 1989).

17. Blu Greenberg, "Zero Population Growth: Feminism and Jewish Survival," *Hadassah Magazine* (October 1978): 12–33. Excerpted from *On Women and Judaism* (Philadelphia: Jewish Publication Society, 1979).

18. Jay Brodbar Nemzer, "Divorce in the Jewish Community: The Impact of Jewish Commitment," *Journals of Jewish Communal Service* 61 (Winter 1984): 150–59.

19. Rabbi Nahum Josephy, executive vice-president of the Rabbinical Alliance of America and secretary of its rabbinical court, quoted in Ben Gallob, "Divorce Among Orthodox on Rise," *The Jewish Advocate,* 17 July 1975.

20. See Gary A. Tobin and Ingrid Lomfors, "The Feminization of Poverty among Jews," unpublished manuscript, Center for Modern Jewish Studies; Lenore J. Weitzman, "The Economics of Divorce: Social and Economic Consequences of Property, Alimony and Child Support Awards," *UCLA Law Review* 28 (November 1981); Ellen Max, "Divorce Is a Financial Disaster for Women and Children," *The Women's Advocate* (September 1982).

21. "Single Parents Demand Services," *The Jewish Advocate,* 3 May 1984; see also Saul Hofstein, "Perspectives on the Jewish Single-Parent Family," *Journal of Jewish Communal Service* (Spring 1978): 236.

22. Frank Mott and Joyce Abma, "Contemporary Jewish Fertility: Does Religion Make a Difference?" *Contemporary Jewry* (1994).

23. For explorations of this complicated issue see: U.S. Bureau of the Census, 1990. Current Population Reports, P-20 no. 436, *Marital Status and Living*

Arrangements: March 1989 (Washington, D.C.: U.S. Government Printing Office, 1989); Current Population Reports, P-20 no. 436, *Fertility of Americans: June 1988* (Washington, D.C.: U.S. Government Printing Office, 1988); Current Population Reports, P-20 no. 428, *Educational Attainment in the United States: March 1987 and 1986* (Washington, D.C.: U.S. Government Printing Office, 1987); and Smeltz and DellaPergola, "Demographic Consequences," 154.

24. Calvin Goldscheider and Frances Kobrin Goldscheider, "The Transition to Jewish Adulthood: Education, Marriage, and Fertility," paper for the 10th World Congress of Jewish Studies (Jerusalem, August 1989), 17–20.

25. Mott and Abma, "Contemporary Jewish Fertility."

26. For a more complete discussion of this issue, see Sylvia Barack Fishman, *A Breath of Life: Feminism in the American Jewish Community* (New York: Free Press, 1993), 45–64.

8

Presbyterian:
Home Life as Christian Vocation
in the Reformed Tradition

WILLIAM R. GARRETT

The Reformed tradition—from Calvin, through the Puritans, to present-day Presbyterians in North America—has experienced a lively and complex relationship to the intensifying forces of modernity, especially insofar as issues pertaining to family life are concerned.[1] With the unleashing of these forces during the early decades of the twentieth century, Presbyterians immediately found themselves drawn into the vortex of those controversies pertaining to the scientific challenges to theological orthodoxy, as well as to the moral strife relating to family matters occasioned by liberalized lifestyles. For the most part, during the 1920s, the conservatives carried the day in the struggle against the pernicious effects of modernized cultural trends when Presbyterian General Assemblies vigorously opposed most modifications in family lifestyle patterns.

The resurgence of liberalized patterns of behavior prompted by the emergence of the counterculture in the 1960s precipitated a decidedly different response from Presbyterians than that exacted in the first round of combat with liberalism in the 1920s. As members of the liberal mainline establishment of American Protestantism, Presbyterians sought to accommodate the demands for women's liberation, premarital sexual experimentation, abortion, the rising divorce rate, the emergence of pluralist family forms, and a succession of other significant changes dramatically revamping the character of American family life in the post–World War II era. Moreover, the strategy of adapting to secular familial changes has remained a feature of Presbyterian life from the late 1950s to the present.

Presbyterians in the 1920s had reacted with considerable dismay against what they perceived to be a deplorable moral deterioration of family life. However, after the mellowing influence of several decades of affluence following World War II, Presbyterian leaders and laity responded with empathy, if not outright approbation, to a new round of liberated lifestyles sponsored by the counterculture. A curious consequence of this approval and support extended to the counterculture's innovations manifested itself in the religious behavior of the baby-boomer generation. The members of this generation failed to return to the ranks of organized religion, and especially to Presbyterian churches, once they had reached maturity and childbearing age. Thus, the last section of this analysis will deal with various issues pertaining to the baby-boomer generation, their family situations, and the likely success of Presbyterian strategies for drawing this generation back into the church.

Calvinism and the Emergence of the Modern Family

The Reformed understanding of marriage and family begins with Calvin's insistence that husband and wife were bound by an ethical obligation to love one another as a form of Christian vocation.[2] Indeed, Calvin specifically cited the idea of companionship between spouses as that most pleasing to the author of marriage. From this relationship it followed, Calvin reasoned, that parents should not only love their children but should also manifest that love through careful nurturing and ongoing attention to their physical and spiritual needs.

Within subsequent Calvinist, and later Puritan, communities, this model of marital relations attained institutionalization over time and was reflected in a succession of other decisive changes in family matters. For example, in the seventeenth century, marriages were still arranged among Puritans in New England, but youth swiftly learned that they merely had to express doubts about being able to love the parental choice and that person would almost certainly be eliminated as a prospective spouse. Parents were loath to place one of their children in a position where God's commandment to love one's husband or wife could not be fulfilled. Calvinist and Puritan groups also countenanced more grounds for divorce than most other religious groups of the time. The mandate for love to prevail between spouses also resulted in a much greater degree of equality between husband and wife than was typical elsewhere in the Euro-American domain. Accordingly, one could argue that the modern family system was a latent consequence of Calvinist theology with its emphasis on romantic attachment as a basis for marriage, on the appropriateness of companionship between husband

and wife, on the propriety of husband and wife equality, on the need for a child-centered nuclear family, in the liberalization of divorce proceedings, and in its gradual erosion of the foundations of the arranged-marriage system.

The Presbyterian Rejection of Modernity in the 1920s

Although selected aspects of the modern age can be traced back to forces unleashed in the Reformation, by the 1920s modernization dynamics crystallized into a new plateau of development by combining with a variety of purely secular influences—industrial, urban, bureaucratic, technological, and intellectual—all of which created a formidable challenge to religious beliefs and practices. Scientific and historical scholarship thrust forward troublesome issues for biblical and theological orthodoxy, whereas the lifestyle innovations placed in jeopardy the moral heritage embodied in family life.

Both the southern (PCUS) and northern (PCUSA prior to 1958 and UPCUSA thereafter) Presbyterians responded to these challenges with varying degrees of alacrity. The northern church exhibited considerably more concern over social issues and entered into a more volatile debate over theological matters than did the PCUS.[3] Internal conflict was not a new experience for American Presbyterians, of course, because they had established a long history of struggle over such divisive issues as revivalism, the theory of evolution, historical criticism of biblical texts, and the social gospel movement whose adherents attempted to move the churches toward a more liberal assessment of and response to the problems occasioned by immigration, urbanization, and industrialization.[4]

General Assembly minutes for the PCUSA also reflect a rising concern in the 1920s and 1930s over such issues as Christian marriage, the grounds for divorce, remarriage, birth control, and moral decline. A Commission on Marriage, Divorce, and Remarriage, reporting in 1930, decried a situation wherein "prophylactics have taken the place of conscience" and such ancillary notions as "if you can't be good, be hygienic" or "let your opportunity be your guide." Although commission members admitted that these views had not become dominant, they were regarded as sufficiently prevalent in contemporary social life to warrant concern on the part of church members. The antidote to the noxious effects of more explicit sexual themes in music, in the "talkies," in fiction, and in magazines was to intensify denominational efforts aimed at bolstering the Christian home and educating youth more proficiently in the ethics of Christianity.

Since the conservative South was less affected by the bohemian culture that altered lifestyles in the North, the PCUS did not begin to address problems associated with divorce, remarriage, and what would now be called family values until the middle of the 1940s. It is clear, however, that both major Presbyterian bodies viewed modernization as an enemy to be stringently opposed on both intellectual and cultural fronts. Northern Presbyterians, in particular, regarded the two domains as intimately connected, with both the Christian home and the family altar considered to be bulwarks against a doctrinal erosion of the faith and a moral decline in personal behavior.

Presbyterians and Family Life:
The Postwar Years

The phrase, "the aberrant fifties," best describes that elongated decade (1946–1964) when American society entered a phase dominated by familism, religiosity, and political conservatism.[5] The liberal lifestyle currents stirring through the first three decades of the century were put on hold—first by the Depression and then by World War II—and they failed to resurface after the war as might have been expected. Indeed, normality returned around 1965 when the counterculture emerged to reappropriate the agenda of the earlier social activists of the 1920s. Meanwhile, during the cultural lull of the 1950s, Presbyterian membership grew at a greater rate than normal population growth, new churches were built in the suburbs as members of the middle class retreated from the inner cities to the green belt, a higher than average growth in income was enjoyed, and a higher degree of education was completed at a rate exceeding the national average of the population.[6]

The result was upward social mobility, and it contributed markedly to a liberalization of Presbyterian theological and moral stances during the 1950s. As in the past, northern Presbyterians mellowed toward liberal manifestations of modernity more readily than their southern Presbyterian counterparts. The PCUSA began revising its conceptions of marriage, divorce, and remarriage in the 1930s, with subsequent revisions enacted in the late 1950s and early 1960s. It was not until the late 1940s, however, that the PCUS broached the whole issue of updating the church's stance toward the secular trend of an increasing divorce rate. Indeed, the opening round in this PCUS reevaluation of marriage, divorce, and related family matters took the curious form of a General Assembly admonition in 1945 that the voluntary *refusal* of married couples to have a reasonable number of children was contrary to the divine purposes of marriage, an admonition that was swiftly proved superfluous since it coincided with the unexpected onset of the baby boom (1946–1964)—although this PCUS pronouncement was certainly not the precipitating cause of that demographic phenomenon.

Meanwhile, the overall cultural tranquility of the fifties provided an atmosphere wherein both Presbyterian communions could revise their earlier and more hostile assessments of modern culture. Sociologist Benton Johnson traced the waning prohibitions on observance of the Sabbath over the course of the twentieth century as an index of the liberalizing trend toward cultural accommodation among Presbyterians, but one could just as easily have used changing attitudes toward divorce and remarriage as a measure of the emergence of a more ameliorating *rapprochement* toward modern cultural patterns.[7] Throughout the decade of the fifties, as the PCUS wrestled with the vexing issues of divorce and remarriage, denominational leaders consistently warned that the church should strive to chart a course between "Pharisaism" on the one hand and the modern trend toward *temporary* marriage on the other. The General Assembly also recognized that the traditional grounds for divorce—adultery and willful desertion—would no longer suffice as cogent church policy, since such a legalistic adherence to tradition would undoubtedly alienate a significant portion of the membership, whose divorce rate was rising along with that of the general population.

By the early 1960s, a whole host of family-related matters crowded the agendas of both the northern and southern churches: premarital and extramarital sex, pornography, the physical and spiritual nature of sexuality, the need for premarital counseling, the appropriateness of planned parenthood, and the moral probity of sterilization of the criminally insane and the mentally impaired (an issue never definitively decided by the General Assembly of the PCUS).

Another salient development was the trend away from "proof texts" drawn from isolated passages of scripture to reinforce the church's stance on these issues. Instead, reports to the General Assemblies recommended that when addressing familial and sexual issues Presbyterians give due weight to the implications derived from the whole panoply of social teachings developed by Jesus. This subtle change in moral direction laid the foundation for dealing with a sweeping set of cul-

tural/moral considerations thrust on Presbyterians in the years immediately following the emergence of the counterculture.

The Counterculture, Baby Boomers, and Presbyterian Family Life Today

The countercultural revolution led by youth in the mid-1960s took many forms—some political in opposition to the Vietnam War and cold war anticommunism; some social and related to equity issues like racism, sexism, and gay liberation; and still others addressing a plethora of lifestyle changes. The sexual revolution, as a part of the larger radical upheaval, constituted not only an attack on the conservative morality of the 1950s but also a rejection of the idealized model for staid middle-class family life with its images of father as breadwinner and mother as homemaker. "Alternative lifestyles" emerged as the fashionable expression for a succession of behavioral patterns introduced during the 1960s such as cohabitation, homosexual unions, premarital sexual activity, open marriage, childless marriage, dual-income couples, and a wider social acceptance of liberalized sexual codes and conduct both inside and outside marriage. The Presbyterian response to this second sexual revolution was markedly different from that extended toward the first. Accommodation now supplanted the more strident hostility that had characterized the church's reactions to the changes of the 1920s.

Ethical reflection also took a dramatic turn during the 1960s. Advocates for the "new morality" downplayed resorting to moral absolutes in devising an ethical stance toward countercultural innovations and advocated considering situational (Joseph Fletcher) and contextual (Paul Lehmann) factors in their stead. Even the more conservative PCUS commended to its membership that they study the questions framed by the leading proponents of the "new morality," although no General Assembly action was taken to approve this controversial approach.

Perhaps the most interesting feature of this stance is that it reflected a more moderate approach to liberal cultural elements than had been in evidence earlier in Presbyterian experience. Indeed, Randall Balmer and John R. Fitzmier, authors of *The Presbyterians,* contend that by the middle of the turbulent sixties Presbyterians began to reassess their traditionally anchored attitudes from a decidedly conservative perspective, undergoing a dramatic change of consciousness with respect to familial, political, and a whole range of social and cultural issues.[8] Presbyterians were influenced in part by the experience of missionaries who felt the brunt of critiques of American cultural imperialism and in part by ecumenical participation with members of other mainline denominational bodies. The socioeconomic strata occupied by American Presbyterians was one of the most important factors influencing change. Although some highly educated members deserted the denomination for more conservative religious bodies, the majority stayed with the Presbyterian communion, struggling to find new ways to relate to the changing cultural scene of the late 1960s and early 1970s. The changing perspective was reflected in the increasing number of ordained women clergy and the programs designed to overcome gender biases in other sectors of the church. The most troublesome case for testing the depths of commitment to the UPCUSA's newfound liberalism was the decision to contribute $10,000 to the Angela Davis defense fund in 1971.[9] Although many members of the denomination contested the wisdom of supporting a political activist like Angela Davis, many black and female members of the church took heart in the symbolic significance of the church's action.

In the throes of contending with the secular cultural agenda of late modernity, Presbyterians also entered into discussions over the merger of the southern and northern branches of the church. Theological, sectional, and confessional disparities obstructed the path, but in 1983 the two branches formalized their reunion to create the Presbyterian Church (USA). While this solved some organizational problems, the merger did not redress what was emerging as a major source of difficulty for the denomination—its sharp decline in membership. In contrast to the marked growth in membership in the 1950s, the 1970s showed an extensive erosion of membership. That pattern has persisted into the 1990s.

Numerous explanations have been advanced to account for the precipitous drop in membership for Presbyterian and other mainline denominations. The key, it seems, lies with the baby-boomer generation. In the past, a pattern of dropping out of organized religion during the collegiate and early adult years, then reaffiliating with religious organizations in generous numbers during the early adulthood and childrearing years was established. However, baby boomers in general did not follow the pattern of previous generations, and a high number of Presbyterian "boomers" in particular failed to return to the ranks of Presbyterianism. According to data gathered in a major study of Presbyterian baby boomers, undertaken by Professors Dean Hoge, Benton Johnson, and Donald Luidens, only 52 percent of all confirmands remained churched—that is, they both held church membership and attended at least six times a year—and among these confirmands 29 percent remained Presbyterian, 6 percent switched to a fundamentalist church, 10 percent affiliated with another mainline denomination, and 7 percent joined a nonmainline church.[10]

These data revealed several striking features. Slightly over half of the current boomers had at one point dropped their religious affiliation. Children and their religious education were central among their reasons for returning.[11] Boomers also reported that they found social and cultural reinforcement for their families in the community of the church, as well as an opportunity for developing rapport with people of similar interests and beliefs. It is curious, however, that parents of the baby-boomer generation, especially the "lay liberals," were considerably less likely than previous generations to impose their particular religious beliefs on their children. They were more concerned that their children develop some religious convictions than that they select the "right" religious beliefs.[12]

The study also shows that religion was rarely a topic of discussion in the families of baby boomers. Active church participation apparently did not result in familial Bible study, devotions, or prayer sessions—other than grace at meals, which was still practiced on those occasions when the family shared a meal together. Gone, however, was the earlier tradition of the family altar that was ardently promoted by Presbyterians throughout the eighteenth, nineteenth, and early twentieth centuries. These results reveal a lower level of commitment to the faith and a reduced sense of commitment to the national denomination.

The heart of religion for the baby-boomer generation seems to adhere somewhat more to moral sentiments than to theological beliefs, since the latter are highly pluralist among Presbyterian baby boomers and autonomously framed by individual believers. Indeed, Wade Clark Roof, author of *A Generation of Seekers,* discerns a correlation between the new family types—blended, single-parent, gay, dual-worker families, and so forth—and greater religious individualism in contemporary American society.[13] Blended families, for example, are 35 percent less religiously homogamous than first-marriage families, so that children are thrust into a situation where they often must decide for themselves with which religious community represented in the household, if any, they will affiliate. Although the Hoge, Johnson, and Luidens' survey did not connect the pluralization of family forms with a greater pluralization of beliefs among those in their Presbyterian sample, it did demonstrate that a wider range of beliefs and a more diversified number of family forms are more evident in this than in previous generations. Baby boomers are more likely to exhibit an openness to points of view that challenge Presbyterian orthodoxy; they are more cosmopolitan, ecumenical, supportive of critical scholarship even when it undercuts specific traditions of the church, more accepting of differing lifestyle choices, sensitive to gender and ethnic differences, less enamored with authority (both civil and religious), and less inclined to follow rules pertaining to dress, alcohol consumption, sexual behaviors, and Sunday observance than Presbyterians of previous generations. Many of these modifications in attitudes and behaviors occurred without formal General Assembly sanctions and many issues that earlier had been the subject of General Assembly concern simply passed by the board without further engagement, producing a kind of tacit acceptance by default.

This is not to say, of course, that family issues no longer matter to Presbyterian leaders or laity. Presbyterian constituents still contend with the troublesome questions surrounding abortion, the fragmentation of family life by divorce, the role of women in church and society, gay rights, the nurturing of children, premarital pregnancy, and a succession of other family problems. But the PC(USA) distances itself from these disputed subjects and from the positions articulated by the New Religious Right with its putative commitment to family values.

Indeed, the PC(USA) seems to have relinquished any desire to try to impose a singular paradigm for family life on its affiliated members. Rather, the Congregational Ministries Division of the denomination has taken the position—based on a study paper presented to the General Assembly of the PC(USA) in 1989, which reminded constituents that the family is the basic building block of the faith community—that the church should provide a community of support, nurture, and growth for families "of all types": single persons, married couples with children, married couples without children, single parents with children, blended families made up of parents and children from previous marriages, unmarried couples, and two adults of the same sex living together.[14] The explicit message suffused through the publications of the Congregational Ministries Division is that local churches should foster an atmosphere of acceptance relative to families and households of all types and devise programs to meet their needs in times of stability, change, or transition.

Absent from this stance is any suggestion that household forms featured in local congregations could be normatively deviant or contrary to biblical teaching. From this perspective, the focus of ministry should be on helping members function more proficiently in whatever household style they have adopted. In other words, congregational attention should be directed toward addressing the emotional, social, and spiritual needs of individuals and families rather than attempting to launch a program to reform households in light of some normative paradigm predicated on the social teachings of the faith. Such a strategy irrevocably relegates to the realm of personal moral decision making the question of what family forms are consistent with religious rectitude and spiritual vitality.

Conclusion

The early twentieth century ushered in a wide succession of liberalized lifestyle changes that challenged established sexual mores, gender roles, and family forms. Presbyterians adopted a reactionary stance that affirmed the probity of traditional family patterns and practices. Utilizing scriptural and doctrinal resources, they vehemently opposed bohemian cultural trends that threatened to erode the old paradigm relative to appropriate family lifestyles and organizational forms. And through it all, Presbyterians remained convinced that the faith spoke directly to what the family should and should not be, as well as how family members should and should not act.

The counterculture in the mid-1960s exacted a quite different response from Presbyterians. Accommodation rather than opposition to liberal forces became the new strategy. Thus by the time the baby-boomer generation had begun to reach its childbearing years, Presbyterians had largely forsaken any attempt to transform family patterns in conformity with some normative model, opting instead to develop ministries that related to the spiritual needs of its members, regardless of the family forms its members embraced.

Whether the current strategy will succeed remains a matter of considerable speculation. Author Dean Kelley has argued cogently that when churches demand little in the way of belief and practice, their membership soon begins to decline.[15] Hoge, Johnson, and Luidens found considerable support for Kelley's thesis in their study of Presbyterian baby boomers, and they have suggested that Presbyterian openness and accommodation to cultural change has left many confirmands with little reason to invest much loyalty in the denomination, apart from their commitment to a local congregation whose ministry effectively meets their needs. Presbyterians appear, therefore, to be caught on the horns of a rather insidious dilemma. To strengthen the core beliefs of the denomination in an effort to allay membership loss will almost certainly require taking a judgmental stance against several alternative lifestyles now featured in their congregations, whereas accommodation to the new familial forms will almost certainly be taken as an indication that the faith has little of importance to say to contemporary family members. Confronted with this conundrum, one can predict with considerable confidence that Presbyterians will proceed in the near future with their strategy of accommodation. They will strive to develop ever more effective ministries to meet the needs of congregants in diverse households. Although considerable risk attends this strategy, it may prove to be the most viable for contemporary Presbyterians in this culturally tumultuous world.

NOTES

1. The author wishes to thank Professor Benton Johnson for his assistance in this research, specifically for his detailed notes pertaining to General Assembly minutes, as well as several articles he produced on Presbyterian life in relation to modernity. He, of course, is not responsible for any errors in fact or judgment contained in this chapter.
2. See in this connection, John Calvin, *Institutes of the Christian Religion,* 2 vols. (Philadelphia: The Westminster Press, 1960); John Calvin, *New Testament Commentaries: Galatians, Ephesians, Philippians, and Colossians* (Grand Rapids: Wm. B. Eerdmans Publ. Co., 1965), 204–9; and for a more detailed presentation of this argument, see William R. Garrett, "The Protestant Ethic and the Spirit of the Modern Family," unpublished paper presented at the Association for the Sociology of Religion annual meeting, Los Angeles, Calif., August 4–6, 1994.
3. Benton Johnson, "From Old to New Agendas: Presbyterians and Social Issues in the Twentieth Century," in *The Confessional Mosaic: Presbyterians and the Twentieth Century,* ed. Milton J. Coalter, John M. Mulder, and Louis B. Weeks (Louisville, Ky.: Westminster/John Knox Press, 1990), 208–35; and Randall Balmer and John R. Fitzmier, *The Presbyterians* (Westport, Conn.: Praeger, 1994), 83–95.
4. Robert Wuthnow, "The Restructuring of American Presbyterianism: Turmoil in One Denomination," in *The Presbyterian Predicament: Six Perspectives,* ed. Milton J. Coalter, John M. Mulder, and Louis B. Weeks (Louisville, Ky.: Westminster/John Knox Press, 1990), 27–48; and Nathan O. Hatch, *The Democratization of American Christianity* (New Haven, Conn.: Yale University Press, 1989), 60–62.

5. See Arlene Skolnick, *Embattled Paradise: The American Family in an Age of Uncertainty* (New York: Basic Books, 1991), 49–53; and Andrew Cherlin, *Marriage, Divorce, Remarriage* (Cambridge, Mass.: Harvard University Press, 1981), 34–44.

6. Dean R. Hoge, Benton Johnson, and Donald A. Luidens, *Vanishing Boundaries: The Religion of Protestant Mainline Baby Boomers* (Louisville, Ky.: Westminster/John Knox Press, 1994), 4–7; Balmer and Fitzmier, *The Presbyterians*, 97–98; and Wade Clark Roof, *A Generation of Seekers* (San Francisco: Harper Collins, 1993), 42–44.

7. Benton Johnson, "On Dropping the Subject: Presbyterians and Sabbath Observance in the Twentieth Century," in *The Presbyterian Predicament*, ed. Coalter, Mulder, Weeks, 90–108.

8. Balmer and Fitzmier, *The Presbyterians*, 100–101.

9. See David B. McCarthy, "The Emerging Importance of Presbyterian Polity," in *The Organizational Revolution: Presbyterians and American Denominationalism*, ed. Milton J. Coalter, John M. Mulder, and Louis B. Weeks (Louisville, Ky.: Westminster/John Knox Press, 1992), 279–306.

10. Hoge et al., *Vanishing Boundaries*, 70–73.

11. Similar findings to those of Hoge, Johnson, and Luidens were discovered by Roof in his study of the religious experiences of the baby boomer generation. See Roof, *A Generation of Seekers*, 156–57.

12. Hoge et al., *Vanishing Boundaries*, 119.

13. Roof, *A Generation of Seekers*, 225–29.

14. David Wasserman and Ray Brugler, *Family Ministries: A Planning Guide for Congregations* (Louisville, Ky.: Christian Education Program Area, Congregational Ministries Division, Presbyterian Church (USA) 1993), vii.

15. Dean M. Kelley, *Why Conservative Churches Are Growing* (New York: Harper & Row, 1977).

9

United Church of Canada: Kingdom Symbol or Lifestyle Choice

DAPHNE J. ANDERSON
TERENCE R. ANDERSON

"We believe that it is our duty as disciples and servants of Christ . . . to preserve the inviolability of marriage and the sanctity of the family."[1] So states one of the Articles of Faith in the United Church of Canada's *Basis of Union,* articles approved in 1925 by the founding churches—Presbyterian, Methodist, and Congregational—when they joined to form the United Church of Canada. How has marriage and the family fared since that time, and, specifically, since 1945?

The post–World War II era in Canada was marked by rapid social change, high immigration, urbanization, and major economic development and prosperity. The population more than doubled to over twenty-seven million. The United Church began this period as the only "made in Canada" denomination, viewed by many as the unofficial "national" church—Mr. and Mrs. Canada. Its membership rose from seven hundred thousand plus to a high of just over a million in 1966. But then its position in Canadian society began to change, and by 1990 it had declined to eight hundred thousand. It is still declining, though it remains the largest Protestant denomination in Canada.

Any comprehensive study of the beliefs and practices of United Church members with regard to the family in this era of change must take into account its diversity. Granted, the United Church was, and is, predominately middle class, white, and anglophone; yet its piety, ethos, and practice reflect Canada's diverse geographic regions with their different religious and cultural histories. Marriage customs and family life vary widely throughout Canada. Family practices in a Newfoundland fishing village congregation of revivalist Methodist roots, for example, are likely to be very different from a university congregation in Toronto with a history of liberal theology, or a congregation founded in the social gospel and frontier climate of an oil boomtown in Alberta. Its diversity also reflects Canada's shift in cultural policy in the 1970s from assimilation of different ethnic groups to affirmation of multicultural-ism. The United Church for years had served as an important gateway into mainstream Canadian society for many immigrants. The church still does not have many ethnic minority congregations. However, it is important to note that whatever generalizations are made about the United Church's beliefs and practices regarding the family may not fit, for example, a Cree congregation in northern Manitoba, or a Japanese-Canadian congregation in Vancouver, or even a Francophone congre-gation in Quebec.

Tracing its history of actual beliefs and practices, then, is beyond the scope of this chapter. We have chosen instead to focus simply on the formal teachings of the United Church regarding marriage and family during this period. This too proved to be no easy undertaking. The United Church has a great variety of such teachings because it is a con-ciliar church with a multilevel democratic system of decision making and authority, plus varied Christian education programs, marriage counseling centers, and family life programs. We have therefore limited our study to the church's commissioned reports that deal with sex, mar-riage, family life, and related subjects. Such reports are commissioned in response to concerns and requests voiced through the various courts of the church. A report is debated by the General Council, the national assembly of the United Church, and then the report and its recom-mendations are voted on. The result is usually a policy declaration, or an approved report recommended for use as a study document by con-gregations and individuals, or both. Occasionally, a report may be shelved as a "historical document." Sometimes no agreement is reached, and the debate continues, possibly for years. The nine reports presented from 1945 to 1990 provide a window—albeit with a limited view—into the United Church concept of family life.[2]

With the exception of the *Manual* and the *Basis of Union*, those reports finally approved by the General Council come as close to "official teach-ing" as anything the United Church has. Even then, the authority granted them is ambiguous. The General Council acknowledges that it may make mistakes and can reverse itself later. The teachings of the reports are not binding on either congregations or members. While some mem-bers will study the reports diligently, others may not be aware that they exist. Nevertheless, they are regarded as expressing the "mind of the church," and certainly they are influential in shaping opinion within it.[3]

What were United Church beliefs and teachings regarding marriage and family in these reports? Did they undergo significant changes over the years? There are some important continuities in the reports, which will be identified. However, the focus of our attention will be a major disjunction between the reports from 1946 to 1975, and those from 1978 forward. A very different theology of sex, marriage, and family, together with a dissimilar assumption regarding the church's moral task, characterizes each of the two sets of reports, thereby marking the fissure between them. We will trace this division and critically analyze its implications for the family.

The authors of this chapter are not distant observers. When the time period under examination began, we had just entered high school. By its end in 1990, we had married, our four children had grown and in turn had married, two were divorced and remarried, and we were blessed with two grandchildren. Throughout this period, we all have been directly involved in some of the internal struggles of the United Church. Our own immediate and wider family as well, then, are part of the subject.

The disjunction that so clearly divides the reports into two clusters does not have to do with differences regarding the way the Bible is used and interpreted, the nuclear family, equality of men and women, or sexuality as a good gift of God, although there are significant variations in emphasis and viewpoint on these key matters. But these differences, while very important, are of such a kind and degree that a recognizable continuity in direction continues throughout the reports. They share, for example, a common operative understanding of family as a household consisting of those members dwelling continuously together. In the dominant cultures of North America, this is usually only a set of parents (or a parent) and children—in other words, a "nuclear family." If both mother and father are present, it is regarded as the "traditional family." As the 1960 report observes, "The modern family does not often include grandparents or older relatives as formerly."[4]

The equality of men and women is another conviction and concern that links all of the reports. In this case, the reports vary, sometimes significantly, as to how equality is understood: equal respect as persons, equal economic opportunities,[5] recognition of the complementary nature of men and women,[6] recognition of the androgynous nature of men and women,[7] and liberation from oppressive structures of patriarchy.[8] There are also important differences in the assessment made regarding the realization of such equality, and the analysis of the cause of inequality.[9] But the commitment to equality remains constant.

All of the reports are also agreed that sexuality, perceived as a powerful life force pervading the whole person, is a good gift of God. This continuity is worth noting because the reports from 1978 on tend to speak as if this idea were a new discovery hitherto suppressed by the entire Christian tradition. True, the lyrical praise for the goodness of sexuality that is found in "In God's Image . . . Male and Female" (1980) is unmatched in the other reports, but similar affirmations are clearly present in each of them.[10]

The disjunction that marks the new direction taken by the reports from 1978 onward concerns two matters: the first, respective theologies of sexuality and marriage; the second, whether standards of sexual expression are a community or a private, individual matter. Both of these discontinuities have profound implications for the United Church's views of the family.

The Purpose of
Marriage and Sexuality

The reports after 1978 narrow the purpose of sexuality and marriage, a divergence from the theology of marriage, sex, and family that distinguishes the pre-1978 reports. In this narrowing of purpose, the essence of both sexuality and marriage is effectively disconnected from procreation and family. The sacramental significance of marriage (as distinct from marriage as a sacrament)—that is that it mediates, however partially and imperfectly, something of the power and presence of God— is virtually absent.

The pre-1978 reports understand Christian marriage to have a threefold purpose. The 1946 document summarizes it as follows: "the lifelong companionship of husband and wife is for the good of each, the welfare of human society, the up building of character, the continuance of the human race, and a preparation for God's Kingdom."[11] The first purpose of marriage is provision for "the hallowing of a lifelong relation" since "man and woman are equally created by God, in God's image and for God's fellowship." The belief that men and women are biologically made for one another and "have need of each other's comradeship" is developed more fully in the 1960 report, in terms of the *henosis* or one-flesh theme found in scripture.[12]

The second purpose is procreation. This flows naturally from the physical intimacy and sexual union that are the spontaneous, happy, and beautiful part of the relationship. "The body operates as the organ of the spirit, and children are the normal and ordained result," says the

1946 report. Men and women are lifted above merely selfish interests by the moral discipline of parenthood. "There may, of course, be Christian marriages which do not issue in children, but *normally,* children are born to bless the home and form another link in the perpetuity of the human race."[13] Procreation, says the 1960 report, "continues the creative activity of God and fulfils the spiritual and physical impulses of the sexual nature of a husband and wife in the begetting of children" (Gen. 1:28).

Finally, marriage is seen as a divine vocation, a calling to provide a family home "whereby God is educating the human race for the coming of his kingdom and the doing of his will." Indeed, such homes and families are symbols of the kingdom of God (a variation on the sacramental theme).[14] They are also essential to the strength and health of the secular state.[15] The 1960 report speaks of the divine vocation of caring for and raising children in "the discipline and instruction of the Lord" (Eph. 6:1,4).[16]

It is within this main agenda—family and marriage—that both reports discuss sex and sexuality. In the words of the 1946 report, God's intention for sex is "both as an expression of abiding love and for the creation of new life."[17] Only in marriage can this be truly realized. A similar twofold purpose of sexual intercourse is found in the 1960 report. Birth control now enables a husband and wife to decide "whether any one act of intercourse shall be for the enrichment of their relationship only, or for the begetting of a child as well." Yet limiting the number of children for purely selfish reasons is regarded as sinful. Christian couples who are unable to have children in the normal manner are encouraged to have a family by adoption.[18] A couple should together make decisions about the number and spacing of children, considering matters of health, prospects for proper care, and the needs of society, especially in view of the population explosion. Sexual intercourse, when it results in procreation, "is a further participation in the creativity of God by the generation of a new person." It will be the sacramental act it is intended to be if "the physical embrace gives effect to an inward and spiritual consummation of love; if it expresses a mutual desire for self-giving as well as for possession; if it expresses wholehearted acceptance and responsibility for one another and for *any outcome of this relationship.*"[19] Christian parents are admonished, then, to accept as a gift of God a child they did not intend to conceive.

The 1975 report, "The Permanence of Christian Marriage," issued by the church's Committee on Christian Faith, belongs with this first set of reports. Again a threefold purpose for marriage emerges. The companionate purpose is primary, but also "the existence of marriage as an institution is directly dependent on the fact that children are the result of bisexual relationships."[20] This time, the "sacramental" purpose of marriage is lifted up more clearly and attributed to the fact that marriage represents "the embodiment of Christ in the church."[21] The vow of permanence in the marriage service is thereby reaffirmed as essential to Christian marriage.

A very different understanding of the purpose of marriage and sexuality emerges in the 1978 report, "Marriage Today: An Exploration of Man-Woman Relationship and of Marriage." In this and subsequent reports the purpose of marriage is reduced to a single objective, companionship now described in terms of intimacy. The purpose of sexuality is disconnected from procreation and family. A sacramental dimension of marriage or sexuality is virtually absent.

"Marriage Today" and "In God's Image . . . Male and Female" (1980) are reports commissioned by the Division of Mission in Canada (a department of the church's national office). The 1978 report was asked to examine "marriage and alternative styles"; the 1980 report (with three of the same members) was to study human sexuality. "In God's Image," especially, was used widely throughout the church as a study document in preparation for the policy decisions formulated in the 1984 document, "Gift, Dilemma and Promise," which was approved that year by the General Council. The 1978 report is worth careful scrutiny because of the way it frames the issues and its general approach and position, setting the direction and tone of the subsequent reports and, ultimately in 1984, the policy of the church. What, then, is the view of marriage and sex espoused by the 1978 and 1980 reports? What, if any, significant modifications were made in the 1984 policy document, "Gift, Dilemma and Promise"?

Self-fulfilment through an intimate relationship is the central focus of "Marriage Today." Intimacy is described as "the process of discovering another—and oneself—to be lovable, trustworthy, stimulating, joyous, beautiful. Intimacy is to experience oneself as deeply companioned and unshakably supported."[22] Marriage, sex, homosexuality, and the like are viewed in terms of their relationship to intimacy. Marriage is not a prerequisite for intimacy. However, the "intention of permanence" provides marriage with a "secure structure that invites and supports intimacy." Hence it "offers *unique* advantages to those who covet *intimacy at its best.*"[23] "In God's Image" confines its discussion of marriage to a reprint of this 1978 piece on intimacy.

The sacramental dimension of marriage is rejected as having "little basis in the Bible" and placing "more sacral weight upon marriage than it is able to bear." The report continues, however: "If marriage is the most intimate and therefore demanding garden for the germination and growth of trust as the very embodiment of faith, then marriage is one of God's most special places for the hearing and incarnating of the Gospel in human life."[24] This suggestion of sacramental meaning, however, does not really impact the overall vision of marriage offered by the report.

Procreation is not included by the report as one of the purposes of marriage. Nor is it mentioned as one of the purposes of sex. The meaning and purpose of sexual intercourse are only what we assign to them, and this obviously will vary. Sexual intercourse, then, has neither intrinsic meaning nor God-given purpose. It may or may not contribute to intimacy; it is not necessary for intimacy. From the viewpoint of the report, the most that can be said about sexual intercourse is that its nature *allows* "it to be an eloquent expression of intimacy," and *sometimes* intimacy "presses towards intercourse for its own expression and confirmation; and intercourse *can* materially assist in the growth of intimacy."[25]

"In God's Image," with its more extensive discussion of human sexuality, generally follows this view. Its chapter on sexuality and the Bible, for example, makes no mention of procreation, children, and family clans concerned with lines of descent.[26] In the conclusion of this 1980 report, however, there is a reference to procreation. "Sexuality *contributes* to two of the most profound human experiences in which we cooperate with God: procreation, the giving of birth to new life; and unity, the growth in wholeness as we grow into loving relationships, becoming whole persons in community."[27] There is no evidence that this lone acknowledgment of procreation has any impact on the rest of the report.

Whether or not to have children is merely a "lifestyle" choice, an example of many such choices facing couples.[28] Even in the report's discussion of why couples may wish to endure pain and difficulty in order to stay together, children, or the trauma such problems may induce in children, are disregarded. The only mention of vocation is the recommendation that some vocation or community service *outside* of marriage will serve intimacy by mitigating its tendency to becoming stifled by its own self-preoccupation.[29]

Both reports exhibit interest in children and family only insofar as they affect the intimacy of couples or the role of sex in fostering it. "In God's Image" only briefly refers to children as catalysts for potential conflict within marriages.[30] Likewise, families are discussed only in terms of their role in shaping attitudes that may later be a source of conflict with a partner in an intimate relationship. In the 1980 report, family love and nurture are mentioned as keys to unlocking the ability to trust, so essential for intimacy.[31] This report does go on to note the alarming epidemic of births to teenage, unmarried mothers. However, it perceives no challenge from this to its view that sex is for unitive purposes only. Rather, this rash of births is ascribed to "our fears and ignorance" that "prevent our schools from teaching sexuality well."[32]

"Gift, Dilemma and Promise" (1984) represents, as much as any document can, the current policy and teachings of the United Church of Canada on this subject. It was given general approval by the thirtieth General Council in 1984. It drew on not only the two preceding reports discussed above, but also on "Faith and Sexuality," a commissioned collection of personal statements on the theology of human sexuality selected to reflect "the range of theological and ethical opinion in this area." In addition, the responses by individuals and groups to "Image of God," collected and analyzed over a three-year period, were taken into account. Modifications made by the General Council before final approval was given to the report are incorporated.

Does this key report carry forward the general viewpoint that characterizes the previous two, one that diverges so sharply from the pre-1978 reports? In terms of the theology of sexuality, marriage, and family life, the answer, on the whole, is yes. Nevertheless, careful reading reveals some modifications.

First, there is some recognition that human sexuality may entail reproduction. "The traditional biological argument suggesting that our survival as a species depends on the urge to reproduce ourselves," is a view that persists in our society, the report acknowledges. This view may complement rather than compete with other views that emphasize the pleasure of sex or claim that "sex tends itself, in a special way, to be communication of deep caring and commitment."[33] In addition, it is admitted, contrary to the 1978 report, that "clearly, procreation, pleasure and commitment all play their part in the relationship between Abraham and Sarah and, by implication, in the general view of the Old Testament towards sexuality" (Gen. 18:12). The Old Testament emphasis on procreation is quickly explained away, however, as due to "the political situation of Judaism in those days when the issue of survival was uppermost." The strongest indicator of a modification regarding the purpose of sexuality comes in one of the seven core policy statements, "acknowledgments and affirmations about sexuality." Sexuality "in its life-enhancing, non-exploitive forms is a primary way of relating to ourselves and to one another *and is the way God has chosen to continue the human race.*"[34]

Another modification from the 1978 and 1980 reports is that marriage is now described as "a gift of God through which Christians make covenant with one another and with God."[35] Setting marriage within the framework of the larger covenant of God with creation, points unavoidably to some purpose and vocation in marriage wider than self-fulfilment through intimacy. And there is a slight indication that the report recognizes this. For example, we read that marriages "reflect an opening out that embraces life and seeks to serve more than its own ends. Love and caring in these families will extend to others and be expressed in some form of effort on behalf of the larger community."[36] In addition, a hint of the "sacramental" significance of marriage appears: "Partners in such a marriage are themselves part of something bigger than themselves. Their marriage takes on new depth and spiritual dimension."[37] However, this turns out to be not a mediation of God's grace to the world, but rather only the couple's sense of God's presence in the midst of their struggle to experience genuine intimacy.

There is very little to indicate that this report deviates much from the previous two concerning the purpose of marriage. Has it anything to do with begetting children, nurturing them, and establishing a home that will pass on a way of life? One of the affirmations on marriage says: "In marriage we offer one another the promise of lifelong companionship, rich expression of human affections and sexuality, and nurture for *the* children."[38] This wording stops short of suggesting that begetting children might be an integral aspect of marriage. Four of the other affirmations have to do primarily with marriage understood as intimacy. A telling point is that the affirmation on sexual intercourse in marriage refers only to its unitive function and says nothing about procreation.

In sum, one has to search with care to locate these few qualifications to the position espoused by the 1978 and 1980 reports. The qualifications are not sufficient either in substance or in the weight given them in the report to alter significantly the basic theology of marriage and sexuality that severs procreation, children, and family from the core purpose of marriage and sexuality.

The Church as Moral Community

All the reports indicate that church members were asking for moral clarity, guidance, and leadership from the respective committees or task forces. How is that responsibility envisioned? That question is another vital demarcation between the two sets of reports. The first set interprets the responsibility in terms of a call to articulate a moral vision with clear moral standards to which members would hold themselves accountable in their decisions and actions. This it what it means for the church to be a moral community with a distinctive way of life.

The second set of reports, on the other hand, appears reluctant generally to engage in any such moral enterprise, and to resist it completely in matters of sexual expression. Instead, they see the main task as offering resources to develop the capacity of individual members for clarifying and choosing their own values from which to make moral decisions. The processes set forth to accomplish this do have a place for moral standards, of the kind used to assess consequences or outcomes of actions. The crucial point to observe, however, is that the individual chooses these values.[39] Note that this is quite different from the commonplace understanding that persons must ultimately make their own moral decisions. In these reports, personal choice is extended to include the selection of the criteria that go into making these decisions. This is the approach when it comes to matters of sexual expression. On the other hand, the sections on sexism in the 1980 and in the key 1984 report reflect the earlier view of the church as a moral community. The statements of moral obligation are direct and specific. Four of the five affirmations regarding "Sexism, Society, Self" state these obligations and indicate the kind of general practices that violate them.

How Does the Family Fare?
Critical Reflections

We have been describing the differences that mark the disjunction between the reports from 1946 to 1975 and those from 1978 to the present. How does the family fare in this shift? Not very well. If the new direction taken by the later reports were scrutinized in terms of intimacy or equality of women and men, the situation would be more positive. But regarding the family, there are at least three features of the new direction we observed in the second set of the reports that are negative for the well-being of families. The cumulative effect is the reinforcement and even moral legitimating of increased individuation and privatization of sexuality; a move away from the relationality so central to family. This direction corresponds almost without deviation to the cultural script of liberal, modern societies of this period, a script dominated by opposition to the smothering collectivism of increased bureaucratization of society.[40] Alas, its "answer" is only to maximize personal choice and self-fulfillment. This script, in the opinion of a growing number of observers, is proving destructive to families and to children.[41]

The first negative feature for families in the second set of reports is that they cease to be an object of much attention. The 1946 report is the last major General Council report primarily about the family. It is interesting that in subsequent years of continuing social change, the United Church chose to focus not on the family but on the related subjects of first, marriage, and then, more extensively, sexuality. The result for the family is more than one of neglect. A more important consequence is a displacement of the family from being central to the lens through which marriage, sexual equality, sexual behavior, birth control, divorce, abortion, homosexuality, and a variety of social issues and practices are interpreted and evaluated. In the second set of reports self-fulfilment through intimacy becomes the interpretive and evaluative lens. The view is very different. From the first perspective, for example, strong and faithful families, and the moral standards needed to support them, are the goal. Social dislocation, economic hardship, self-seeking, and permissive sexual practices are the obstacles. The second view sees self-fulfillment in intimacy, and the personal skills and virtues needed for achieving it, as the goal. Conventional morality, institutional marriage, and to a degree, even the family itself are seen as the obstacles. Second, and most important, there are a number of negative implications for the family in the teachings of these reports on marriage and sexuality. We briefly note two such teachings. The one more obviously detrimental to strong and faithful families is the reduction of the purpose of marriage to *only* companionship, interpreted entirely in terms of intimacy. The issue here, of course, is not that couples will not have children; they continue to do so unabated.[42] Nor is it the issue that couples who are unable to procreate, or those who have a special vocation that does not entail raising children, should not be seen to have a rich marriage and legitimate place. Their place should be recognized. Rather, the issue is that when procreation is dropped from the core meaning of marriage, children come to be seen as an optional extra, a personal preference, not central to the regular vocation of marriage. A whole different set of expectations for marriage and family is thereby set in motion. These more self-centered expectations resonate with a consumer-oriented society. Children come to be easily regarded as desirable items that might be nice to have when you are ready for them. Unexpected pregnancies or unwelcome newborns (those "not made to order") are regarded with a sense of betrayal and hostility. Further, the marginalization of procreation in marriage can in turn shape what the church offers to and what it expects from families. The vocation of being "a domestic church" and of struggling with what is entailed in parenting and in passing on a way of life in the midst of the pressures of a secular society simply vanishes from view, as the second set of reports demonstrates.

Another detriment to strong and faithful families is the disappearance of procreation from the purpose of sex. It is ironic that this happens in the reports that are most vocal on embodiment and criticize body and spirit dualism. It is difficult to understand how embodiment could be taken seriously while at the same time ignoring the main biological function of sex in favor of a purely "spiritual" interpretation, the unitive purpose. Of course, improved technology in birth control (the pill) made the separation more feasible, but this is only a matter of degree. As we have seen, birth control was regarded in the earlier set of reports as a more responsible way of begetting and nurturing children, not of reducing the purpose of sex to providing pleasure and serving as a unitive force.

Whatever the explanation for disconnecting procreation not merely from specific acts of sexual intercourse but from the entire purpose of sex, it reflects an important underlying moral change: Bodily acts in themselves are no longer regarded as constituting "personal or moral commitments of the self."[43] Thus sexual intercourse doesn't intrinsically entail any moral commitment, including responsibility for procreation, offering women a rationale for abortion. Today, becoming a mother is not a possibility to which one commits oneself by the act of sexual intercourse. One becomes a mother only if one explicitly consents to become a mother. By the same reasoning, it offers men the rationale to become "deadbeat dads"—those who refuse to support their offspring or accept fatherhood. If one does not explicitly "sign on" for children in any act of sexual intercourse, why should one support any child that may result? We are confronted by ever-increasing abortion rates and by growing numbers of children under the care of single mothers without support.

A third feature with negative impact for strong and faithful families is the virtual moral abdication by the church in the area of sexual expression, especially outside of marriage. Instead of providing a moral vision and standards for guidance, the church asks individuals to make such decisions by themselves. This represents radical "subjectivism" in ethics and, if followed consistently, undercuts the meaning of "moral," since the latter entails by its very nature a communally recognized framework of standards.[44] Such extreme privatization is not countenanced by the church in any other area of life, including other aspects of sexuality and man–woman relations. This combination of a special ethic for sex, and a highly subjectivist one at that, does not foster the kind of moral responsibility required for marriage, parenthood, and faithful families.[45]

The final feature, one that belongs to all the reports not just the second set, has long-term, harmful implications for strong and faithful families: the assumption that "family" means only the nuclear family household. This restriction is both unrealistic and impoverishing. It is unrealistic in that it fails to take account of our connectedness to our relatives who do not live in the same household. A recent study of Canadian families shows that such ties continue to be significant for most Canadians in spite of increased geographic distance between various family members.[46] It is impoverishing because it means that the nature, obligations, and rich possibilities of these bonds are not even explored. What is the Christian calling involved in being related as aunt, uncle, grandparent, cousin, grown sibling, in-law, stepsister, and the like?

There has been a growing trend since the mid-1980s to use "family" to designate any association that performs certain functions—"a secure environment for nurture, growth and development," and the like. This is reflected in a United Church program, "All Kinds of Families," and in a 1988 "shelved" report.[47] Family is now defined as "*two* or more persons who are joined by reason of mutual consent (marriage, *social contract* or covenant) *or* by birth or adoption/placement."[48] In our view, this move is also unrealistic and impoverishing. It is unrealistic because the family is not some abstraction, invented by humans, that can be redefined to suit our purposes. Rather, it identifies a core human experience—the bonds that are entailed in procreation, giving birth, and by extension, other blood ties. The central feature of this connectedness is that it is *given,* not *chosen.* Even marriage and adoption, though partly matters of choice, entail an involuntary aspect. We chose our adopted daughter; she did not choose us. Nor did her siblings, grandparents, uncles, aunts, and a host of other kin have a choice in the matter. We are now connected to our sons-in-law and daughters-in-law and their children and kin by no choice of our own. Everyone has relatives, and they cannot be made to vanish by redefining the family. If the term "family" is used to designate some other kind of entity, another word would have to be invented to name this reality.

Such an effort to redefine the family is impoverishing because it reflects and reinforces the profound disease with "nonchosen" relations that is characteristic of the "hyper-individualism" of modern, Western societies. Rather than deal with the challenge of nonchosen relations, including the distortions that can infect them, the preference is for associations of our own choosing, congenial to our likes and interests, from which we can exit easily if they prove difficult. Deliberately chosen associations, of course, have their own worth and place. Fortunately, some of them can even perform functions similar to families. But they are different from nonchosen forms of connectedness. The difficulty moderns have in dealing responsibly with the latter brings great destruction and grief. The church needs to help us face this and not abet flight to purported substitutes by blurring the differences.

Why Did These "New" Teachings Go Unnoticed?

The most surprising discovery for us in carrying out this inquiry is that the beliefs that we have identified as shaping the new direction taken by the second set of the reports are given no Christian warrant of rationale. They are not even identified by the reports as constituting a significant change. Nor are they lifted up for discussion in the church. Yet these beliefs have major implications for the family. They represent, as we have seen, a significant shift both from the reports of less than a decade earlier and from the entire Christian tradition. Whether these changes should be applauded or should be considered, as we claim, detrimental to strong and faithful families, we are left wondering how they could pass virtually unchallenged and apparently taken for granted.

There was no shortage of controversy and debate over sexuality in the church during these years, but for the most part it centered on issues such as abortion, sexism, homosexuality, and sex outside marriage. The new underlying premises of the second set of reports for the most part escaped attention. Did the "culture of narcissism," generated by a combination of highly individuated persons with affluence and a consumer economy, engulf the church? The second set of reports, especially the 1978 and the 1980 ones, do reflect some narcissistic features. The preoccupation with self-fulfillment, in which love itself comes to be understood in terms of fulfillment of individual freedom and the means to immediate personal gratification, is there. Likewise, the reports manifest strong traces of the popular ideology characteristic of this narcissistic era, an "ideology of non-binding commitments and open-ended relationships—an ideology that . . . condemns all expectations, standards, and codes of conduct as 'unrealistic.'"[49] The strong influence of the widely held synthesis between certain Christian theologies and Rogerian or related therapies (Gestalt, Transactional Analysis) is evident. The synthesis contains a subtle disparagement of all culture and tradition because they are identified with prohibitive super egos and are thus the cause of neurosis.[50] But insofar as this is true, we are still left with the question of why the United Church of Canada was so vulnerable to this "spirit of the age." The answer is no doubt complex and requires more analysis than is possible here. But we offer an observation.

One of the noticeable features of the second set of reports, again in contrast to the first set, is the absence of conversation with either the past tradition of the church, the earlier reports of the United Church itself, or sister churches of the ecumene. As we saw, there is appeal to the Bible, but no reference to the long tradition of Christian engagement with it. Larry Rasmussen believes that a shared history and culture is one of the key requirements for strong communities of moral formation on which liberal, modern societies are so dependent: "We are particular beings rooted in time and place who find our moral identity through a 'narrative' understanding of our lives. We express in our very being the history and the communities of which we are a part. Without them we are morally nowhere."[51] Collective judgment requires a sense of history. Attention to the church's history and conversation with its tradition would have provided much needed perspective on the present, throw into relief proposed basic changes, reveal how much they mirror the times, and aid us in assessing their significance and validity.

We have looked through only one window, the United Church of Canada's "official reports" on sex, marriage, and family, to glimpse its understanding of family since 1945. The view is limited, but significant. As the United Church of Canada moves into a period of renewed interest in the family, we hope it will address the serious concerns that the second set of reports have generated.

NOTES

1. United Church of Canada, *Manual* (Toronto: United Church of Canada Publishing House, 1995).
2. During the period under discussion, a number of such reports regarding sex, marriage, and family life were commissioned, written, and debated.

The key ones for our purpose include "Report of the Commission on Christian Marriage and Christian Home" (1946); the Report of the Commission on Christian Marriage and Divorce, including "Toward a Christian Understanding of Sex, Love and Marriage" (1960) and "Marriage Breakdown, Divorce, Remarriage: A Christian Understanding" (1962); "Gift, Dilemma and Promise," prepared for the General Council of 1984, and interim reports leading up to "Marriage Today" (1978); "In God's Image" (1980) and "Faith and Sexuality" (1981); and "Toward a Christian Understanding of Sexual Orientation, Lifestyles and Ministry" (1988). The 1988 report was not passed by General Council but was received as a historical document, and therefore is not central in our study.

3. "Gift, Dilemma and Promise," 5.
4. "Toward a Christian Understanding of Sex, Love and Marriage," 23, 27.
5. "Christian Marriage and Christian Home," 112.
6. "Toward A Christian Understanding of Sex, Love and Marriage," 25.
7. "In God's Image," 83.
8. "Gift, Dilemma and Promise," 67.
9. "In God's Image," 81. For a deeper analysis of sexism, see "Gift, Dilemma and Promise," 55.
10. See for example, "In God's Image," 4; "Christian Marriage and Christian Home," 132, 135; and "Toward a Christian Understanding of Sex, Love and Marriage," 8.
11. "Christian Marriage and Christian Home," 138.
12. "Toward a Christian Understanding of Sex, Love and Marriage," 1.
13. "Christian Marriage and Christian Home," 110 (emphasis ours).
14. Ibid., 107.
15. Ibid., 110.
16. "Toward a Christian Understanding of Sex, Love and Marriage," 1.
17. "Christian Marriage and Christian Home," 133.
18. "Toward a Christian Understanding of Sex, Love and Marriage," 16.
19. Ibid., 8.
20. "Permanence of Christian Marriage," 1.
21. Ibid., 6.
22. "Marriage Today," 89.
23. Ibid., 91 (emphasis ours).
24. Ibid., 88.
25. Ibid., 91(emphasis ours).
26. "In God's Image," 20. Genesis 4:1 is interpreted without reference to procreation.
27. Ibid., 94 (emphasis ours).
28. Ibid., 100.
29. "Marriage Today," 94.
30. "In God's Image," 20.
31. Ibid., 63.
32. Ibid., 7.

33. "Gift, Dilemma and Promise," 12.
34. Ibid., 19–20 (emphasis ours).
35. Ibid., 36.
36. Ibid., 31.
37. Ibid., 24.
38. Ibid., 36 (emphasis ours).
39. "Marriage Today," 112; "In God's Image," 74. In "Gift, Dilemma and Promise," single persons are given no norms to guide in decisions pertaining to "sexual fulfilment," 54(d).
40. See W. M. McClay, "The Hipster and the Organization Man," *First Things* (May 1994): 23–30.
41. See William A. Galston, "Beyond the Murphy Brown Debate," speech delivered at the Annual Family Policy Symposium of the Institute for American Values, New York, December 10, 1993; and Christopher Lasch, *Haven in a Heartless World* (New York: Basic Books, 1977).
42. *Profiling Canada's Families* (Ottawa: Vanier Institute of the Family, 1994), 52.
43. Gilbert Meilander, "The Eclipse of Fatherhood," *First Things* (June/July 1995): 38.
44. Don Browning, *The Moral Context of Pastoral Care* (Philadelphia: Westminster Press, 1976), 25. Browning regards this kind of abdication as partly due to the confusion about the place of the moral in pastoral care.
45. The "shelved" report, "Toward a Christian Understanding of Sexual Orientation, Lifestyles and Ministry," 57, 63. The report rejects the idea of a special sex ethic and advocates a set of common values.
46. *Profiling Canada's Families,* 126–30.
47. "Toward a Christian Understanding of Sexual Orientation, Lifestyles and Ministry," 59.
48. "All Kinds of Families," 2 (emphasis ours).
49. Lasch, *Haven in a Heartless World,* 140.
50. The following is drawn from Don Browning, "Images of Man in Contemporary Models of Pastoral Care," *Interpretation* 33 (April 1979): 144ff. See also T. R. Anderson, "The Sexuality Report: Another View," *Touchstone* 1 (January 1983): 28–29.
51. Larry L. Rasmussen, *Moral Fragments and Moral Community* (Minneapolis: Fortress Press, 1993), 114.

10

Episcopal:
Family as the Nursery
of Church and Society

JOANNA BOWEN GILLESPIE

"Families are the nurseries of societies and states," declared the *Churchman's Magazine*, the nation's first Episcopal journal, in 1807.[1] Like skillful gardeners, parents were encouraged to tend their seedlings, uprooting noxious weeds, pruning useless branches, and nipping "every opening vice in the bud." And, as the author warned, in a society still crafting its own identity after the American Revolution, religious parents held a sacred mandate: Children who did not learn obedience would "never know how to govern." The duties of citizenship required that young people be trained for "civic competence," the self-mastery and ownership of property that entitled one to freedom and privilege.

This concise expression of the Episcopal family theology in the early Republic grew out of its understandings of rank, responsibility, and initiative, traits embodied by the founding fathers. Though the essayist did not directly employ the concept of "station," he could assume that his readers would not only understand but also embrace it as part of their allegiance to the doctrines of the Great Catechism. Second-generation American Episcopalians carried an almost proprietary view of leadership in a "world turned upside down" by the recent Revolutionary War; indeed, the prospect of "pure family democracy" was, as the author put it, "most alarming."[2] In the early nineteenth century, Episcopalian church rhetoric assumed that the patriarchal family was the primary vehicle for training the young toward their future social responsibilities—males to leadership and females to supportive domestic companionship.

From its beginnings, this domestic theology conflating family, society, and government formed an unexamined bedrock of denominational identity. Indeed, nearly a century after the *Churchman's Magazine* article appeared, Episcopal bishops still named family as the "root germ" of church and society. "The hearth of the home is the sacred altar, at least, of all religion, all law, and all order," their 1892 Pastoral Letter proclaimed. "The awful sacredness of home, the one man and the one woman who are not two but one" must not only people and perfect the human race but serve as earthly symbols of the union between Christ and the church. "When the family is wrecked," they warned, "neither Church nor State is worth preserving."[3]

The Nineteenth-Century Episcopalian Family as Cultural Metaphor

Internal church policies and preachment generally marginalized private sphere concerns, including the family—"the sufferings engendered by war, ecological crises, economic injustice and epidemic disease," even childbirth and childrearing. Episcopal women and children, peripheral to organizational concerns, were granted the status of "privileged subordination" in their church as long as they did not overstep its social expectations.[4]

However, the external public sphere of the state was somehow synchronous with Episcopalians' own sense of order and form. Oft-heard prayers stressed their "positions of responsibility" in a great nation,[5] oft-sung hymn words ("Can we, whose souls are lighted/With wisdom from on high/Can we to men benighted/The lamp of life deny?"[6]) helped them to believe that their church was a "surrogate guardian in matters of a national faith and morals."[7] One nineteenth-century clergyman-historian announced that the Episcopal Church was "becoming what she ought to be, . . . a grand center of moral power, a main source of religious order, of civil obedience and of general prosperity."[8]

Episcopalians saw themselves as symbolizing deep connections between family and church. Good taste was cultivated as a domestic and a godly virtue. An Episcopal culture of order and reverence embodied in the gothic architecture the era offered, in the words of Harriet Beecher Stowe, herself a mid-life convert, "repose for those bruised by Puritanism."[9] Episcopalian church architecture, as historian Richard Bushman has argued, helped create an American Protestant "theology of taste." Congregational theologian Horace Bushnell theologized such refinement as "an expression of godly morals" in which cultivated taste almost became an attribute of God.[10] One young congregationalist wrote that college-bred youth were entering the Episcopal Church "to satisfy their aesthetic, if not their spiritual desires."[11] If individual Episcopalians gave it conscious thought, they believed their church was the highest embodiment of American culture, and the Episcopalian family epitomized the ideal American family. Their church was ritualizer par excellence of family events, the preferred public setting for weddings and funerals in a society yearning for evidence of taste and culture.

Serious, well-educated Episcopal laywomen also maintained ties between home and church by undertaking familial, private-sphere tasks for their congregations. They expressed their version of civic responsibility and community outreach in parish-aid societies, Mothers' Associations, school teaching, Sunday schools, and policy-making on health and public relief commissions.[12] They supplied the actual hands-on work of care giving through the Women's Auxiliary, became deaconesses and presocial work volunteers in the urban settlement-house movement, and undertook children's religious formation within the home.

Yet Episcopal clergy and leadership, though always presuming an understructure of family and home, expended little intellectual capital on it. Despite what might be considered a "feminine" preoccupation with form and taste, the Episcopal Church was an unalterably masculine institution, an identity perpetuated by its theological neglect of the family. A recent denominational study of clergy families observes that it "never had a theology of *married* priesthood, let alone of family."[13] Its hierarchical authority structures historically devalued concerns of the private or feminine sphere as worthwhile objects of theological attention.

Nineteenth-century Episcopalians focused instead on their worship heritage, an inherited structure and liturgy Americanized in terms of more lay authority and participation. One might say that Episcopal liturgy *was* its theology, "Father, Son, and Holy Ghost" its model of family. The great missionary movements of the nineteenth century diffused Episcopal ideals of order and civilization across America. Anglo-Victorian Sunday school literature and popular fiction helped to mythologize the cultural significance of the Episcopal family. Though President Theodore Roosevelt remained loyal to his family's Dutch Reformed heritage, his Anglocentric mind-set led him to view Episcopalianism as "one of the two denominations best suited to America" (the other being Methodism).[14]

Episcopalians in the Twentieth Century

Even after World War I, when divorce became an increasing threat to the infrastructure of marriage and family, Prayer Book liturgy and rubrics about Holy Matrimony (unaltered from its Church of England roots) remained the major source of Episcopal teachings about marriage, family, and community. Following World War II, this situation began to change as a new religious education curriculum implicitly, perhaps unintentionally, updated the old pattern of "family government." The Seabury Series included a strong component of lay-adult education, reflecting the traditional emphasis on instructing the adults to reach the children. A state-of-the-educational-arts curriculum, its theology emphasized individual responsibility and choice. The accompanying volumes of doctrinal summary (*The Episcopal Church's Teaching Series,* published from 1949 to 1961) acknowledged that the denomination made no claim to one unitary "Christian model" of family (even as popular culture resonated to a "Life with Father" stereotype).[15]

The new curriculum inspired a family service, inserted between the usual "early" 8 A.M. Eucharist and the "main" service with choir and candles at 11 A.M., to lure "the entire family" into church at the same time. Previously, Episcopal children were rarely seen in "adult services"; the Sunday school provided "children's worship." Also, at that point, children could not receive communion until they were confirmed (at approximately age thirteen). This innovation of time and focus—welcoming children in a formal church context—quickly became standard practice, even if its concern was increasing numbers at Sunday morning church more than a ministry to parents and families.[16]

Still, the Seabury Series, initiated to enliven the church's "relevance" to young Episcopalians, had its most positive results among lay adults who for the first time in the 1960s received serious theological education. The entire family kneeling together at the communion rail produced a marked change in the culture of many Episcopal congregations. Although children could not receive communion until the 1970s (they were given a blessing instead of bread and wine), the family was participating together in the same religious ritual.

Twentieth-century family theology was also profoundly affected by a second series of developments: denominational discussions of marriage, particularly its capacity to contain sexuality.[17] In 1916, the first Episcopalian study to deal expressly with the family condemned modern attitudes toward divorce and polygamy.[18] As the century progressed, however, canonical procedures changed to accommodate divorce and remarriage within the church. Moreover, Episcopal teaching about marriage itself began to shift: procreation was no longer deemed its sole purpose. By the late 1970s, a Joint Commission of Human Affairs reported a "widening" of acceptable norms of marriage and family. The concept of family as a two-parent nuclear household had become one option among others.[19] Sexuality, no longer embedded in family configurations and the social construction of marriage, pursued its own, more complicated path. Attitudinal shifts regarding sexual decisions during the 1960s had begun to honor individual privacy and autonomy over community expectations. But until the ordination of women brought gender-related issues to the surface in the 1970s, sexuality remained an unacceptable topic for discussion in church.

The gender conflict during the 1960s sparked by discussion of women in ordained roles of deacon and priest has been linked by at least one historian to the emergence of open debate about homosexuality. "Contemporary divisions in the church [and] the current controversies surrounding homosexuality are offshoots of the focus on women and their place in the sacred order; both represent the new pluralism within the church," Katherine Prelinger writes. That debate "required . . . reexamination of [traditional patriarchal] prescriptions concerning body and spirit, fertility and celibacy, [and] the church's role in upholding or subverting societal heterosexual domination."[20] Sexual morality as traditionally defined seemed totally open to question.

The changes did not occur without controversy. Some Episcopalians saw them as an attack by feminists, homosexuals, psychologists, sociologists, and church politicians on the "family" as traditionally defined. An advocacy group for homosexual Episcopalians formed in 1976. Calling itself "Integrity," it represented the other side of the controversy. The 1994 General Convention's Sunday worship service, attended by 8,000 Episcopalians, was picketed by another Protestant denomination with signs proclaiming it the "Fag Church." "God Hates Gays," a sign announced, warning that "Fags Will Burn in Hell." Such responses may well have inspired a *New Yorker* cartoon in which a surpliced Episcopal priest pronounced from his pulpit: "After God had rested on the seventh day, on the eighth day, He said, 'Let there be *problems.*' And *there were problems.*"

One significant point of controversy was the national conference on the family, sponsored by the national Christian Education Department in 1978. A working paper distributed prior to the conference, titled "Today's Families and the Challenges for the Year 2000," aimed at a common starting point for definitions, statistics, and projections. It was deconstructive in tone, declaring its intention to free participants from the mental "trap of nostalgia" for the traditional nuclear family.

Challenging the WASP Episcopal image with the widest possible inclusivity, the paper argued for dismantling gender-role prescriptions. It urged Episcopalians to challenge their unwitting participation in the economic oppression of poor families, and urged openness to multicultural diversity by welcoming people from non-Anglo backgrounds without forcing them to surrender their own cultures. It urged more creative education about the range of family relationships and about sexuality.

The conference itself staged some twenty-nine workshops. A representative sample of titles demonstrates its reach: "Pastoral Models for Strengthening Families"; "The Congregation as a Healing Community"; "Domestic Violence"; "Single Parent Families"; "AIDS"; "Building Families in and for a Multicultural, Multiracial Society"; "Family Ministry in the Gay and Lesbian Community"; Families as Environmentalists"; "Families with Physically Handicapped Members"; Family Members with Developmental Disabilities"; "Homelessness" (a new topic for most Episcopalians); and "Economic Issues in Families" (addressing root causes of problems). Press releases emphasized the conference aims of "transcending" the "limiting ideal of the nuclear family."[21] For Episcopalians uncomfortable with this brave new worldview on "family" and ministries "for the disempowered," traditional rhetoric about family was invisible.

Although budgetary shortages during the 1980s curtailed the national diffusion of conference materials within local parishes, the meeting did result in the formation of an Episcopal Family Network. It issued a study on *The Clergy Family* and began publishing *Family Matters,* a newsletter to assist church leaders with programs, books, and resources. It also published a workbook for children, *Being God's Family.* A number of Episcopal parishes have had some interaction to date with these "new-vision" materials.

The new inclusiveness was reflected in the 1994 General Convention theme, "One God, One Family, One Earth," and was symbolized in its accompanying logo. That design was formed by an abstract representation of hands joined at the wrist, curving out to cup a chalice (incidentally forming lines that could be seen as the genetic sign for the female, and the cross). In the chalice sat a globe, symbolizing both the planet and the consecrated wafer or Host, on which were the profiles of the four human racial archetypes.

Today, the former denominational focus on family delimited by sex and marriage has been subsumed under the broader concept of "the family as a social institution." In public forums as well as seminaries,

Episcopal thinking about family now includes a broad range of kin and non-kin relationships in a variety of racial and economic settings (households). This striking expansion is highly significant in a church that has long equated "family" with "society"—although in terms of actual denominational statistics of rising divorce, single-parent households, and dual-career families, the abruptly universalized metaphor may indeed have been prophetic.

Contemporary Issues in
Episcopalian Family Theology

In this respect, of course, Episcopalians resemble other white, mainline denominations, though with some important differences. A profile of the Episcopal Church today places it sixth in size among Christian denominations after Roman Catholics, Southern Baptists, United Methodists, Evangelical Lutherans, and Presbyterians.[22] Membership peaked at 3.5 million in the anomalous church-going decade of the 1950s. Today it numbers something over 2.5 million, with approximately 15,000 ordained clergy. Its membership, however, is aging. In 1987, 42 percent of its members were over fifty years of age; 92 percent were white; 51 percent were women. In their survey, *American Mainline Religion,* Wade Clark Roof and William McKinney listed Episcopalians, along with Unitarian-Universalists and Jews, as highest on the "status indicators" of achieved levels of education, family income, occupations, and perceived social class. This status accompanies an unconscious mind-set that allows families to take for granted literacy, schooling, cultural experiences, and access to a wide range of information and technology.[23]

It is not surprising that, given this level of educational and cultural privilege, Episcopalians are one of the most socially liberal mainline denominations. They were the first to grant rights to racial minorities and, according to Roof and McKinney, rank third in support of women's rights. They are fifth in accepting or dealing with "new sexual attitudes," the euphemism for conflicts over homosexuality and abortion. Perhaps the most significant denominational feature is its proportion of *adult* converts. The Roof and McKinney survey reports that more than half of its members became Episcopalians after childhood. If, as the survey reports, 68 percent of all Episcopalians have been to college (the same proportion having formal education as among Jews), they can be classified as part of the "knowledge class" in a culture that increasingly equates economic opportunity with schooling.

An interesting anomaly highlighted in that survey is that up to three times as many Americans are likely to "think of themselves as Episcopal" as are listed on actual church rolls. Why this denomination receives a disproportionate amount of nonpracticing support is a logical query. One church journalist thinks it may be because of Episcopal clergy who "dress like Catholics [but] talk like politicians."[24] In modern news media photographic iconography, Episcopalians are a convenient visual representation of Protestantism.

Current views about family among Episcopalians are being shaped by denominational ethicists and theologians. The emerging theology of family sports a new terminology: "household" replaces an outmoded, stereotyped "family," and "covenant" replaces the concept for intentionality and commitment in relationships—both human and divine. One theologian, William Countryman, warns against literal application of the Bible's sexual ethics to today's world; no one can seriously view the gospel as a "system of ideas that can be fully comprehended by anyone *apart from* the necessity of personal transformation."[25] Individualization in American life, he argues, is a central social fact that must be incorporated theologically; in contemporary society people make personal rather than corporate ethical decisions. The "interior good" found in marriage and "other lasting sexual liaisons" is the only way to obviate selfishness, because it places the individual within a relational context.

Countryman also believes that the transition from a familial to an individualist society affects the task of childrearing. The parents' role must be transformed from ownership—seeing the child as an extension of the parent—to education. Nurturing and "leading out" children requires parents' "loving, persistent demand" that children become responsible for themselves, their own choices and relationships, their work, and the world. The institutional church no longer acts as rulegiver, but as a "repository of the sacred," the silent supportive partner to the family. And, when it comes to marriage, Countryman feels that the church may need to wait until a relationship grows before blessing it, rather than establishing a prescriptive starting point in the hope that the ideal relationship will develop and persist. To assume eternal loyalty in marriage when interior trust has not been established, or after it has been broken, violates the concept of marriage and its historic assumptions.

Another contemporary translation of biblical codes, by ethicist Thomas Breidenthal, offers a new perspective on private and public

Christian households, arguing that human fellowship, or "nearness," is *the* great Christian good; a gift of God. Christ comes to *transform* human communities, including households and families, not to deliver people out of them. Only the power of Christ enables physical intimacy or "nearness" in human life to be affirmed and realized, without letting the self become blinded to or irresponsible in the face of its equal potential for evil and damage. "The whole dangerous business of family and household life becomes in Christ an occasion for sanctification of our nearness to one another."[26] Yet another dynamic in the emerging theology of family arises out of the church's belated acknowledgment that Anglo-Episcopal culture in the past has been identified with the dominant more often than with the powerless, both in families and in other societal institutions. African-American Episcopal Bishop Barbara Harris has noted that the Episcopal Church has had an uneasy conscience about racism and other power-imbalance "isms" ever since it began to face its history "as chaplain to the oppressors."[27]

The most comprehensive summary of new, inclusivist teachings about family was a document produced for the 1988 Anglican Bishops Conference.[28] Relocating the starting point for family theology from "sex and marriage" to "the coming kingdom of God," it examined national and community factors for their impact on families around the globe. It called on Anglican churches in all cultures to reexamine their actions against Jesus' model and to strengthen advocacy for the victims of power and abuse *within families* as well as institutions. In direct opposition to a traditional, literal, or fundamentalist position, no one model of family life is mandatory. Christians must remain open to new perceptions, new relationships, and new networks. Community cannot be "imposed." It must grow organically—the local church community that functions as a *substitute* or *auxiliary* set of relationships in meeting the emotional and physical needs of *family*—as an Anglican ideal. The document affirmed the marriage relationship as part of God's creation, but one that must be "redeemed" to promote equality between the sexes, the only ground of true mutuality and fidelity.

Sexuality, it affirmed, must now be understood as "socially constructed," involving much more than genital sex. Individuals are responsible for self-definition and choice. Promiscuity in any relationship, heterosexual or homosexual, is destructive and sinful. "Membership in [a more] open family of grace calls for a new style of living and invites us to renounce traditional ideas regarding privilege, power, and possessions [as well as] to attempt to redress injustice and the structures that perpetuate injustice."

The concept of "open family" might even need to be replaced with "open community," the report concluded, in order to make the new stance definitive. Instead of viewing "the married couple" as a religious icon, single adults become central so that individuals in Christ—the once married, the social outcast, and victims of marital breakdown (including children)—are all equally important. It also affirmed that small groups, communities, or households are *the* effective human fellowship through which Christ's message can be transmitted. Acknowledging the formative role played by small country churches in the lives of present-day adults in city congregations, it honored the intimacy and depth available only in small face-to-face groupings. "For the constant renewal of the city, and the continual vitalization of the city church, serious attention must be given to the *small* community."

Given the breadth and diversity of Episcopal church members, inclusive definitions of family naturally engender dissenting opinions. Displacing the 1950s WASP family icon is only one of several modernizations viewed as dangerous or anti-tradition. The current package of objections most often includes the ordination of women, the modernizing of liturgical language toward contemporary and gender-inclusive imagery in the *Book of Common Prayer* and the *Hymnal,* and any actions that legitimate the status of homosexuality, especially ordaining priests who are open, non-celibate homosexuals.

At the most recent General Convention, the issue of homosexuality topped the dissension list. Churches who had formed a separate entity called the Episcopal Synod of America condemned what they perceived as "the general trend against biblical morality" in the unwillingness of the House of Deputies to condemn ordination of practicing homosexuals. At the same time, however, it urged "all faithful people to stay together" in the Episcopal church, while "being careful to look after their own soul's health."[29] Another more localized example of anxiety about change of tradition surfaced in response to a visual image in a new Episcopal Sunday school curriculum. The "take home" picture card for little children happened to portray, as the illustration of a particular Bible verse, a family, including a mother and several children. This impelled an outraged phone call to the series editor: "Why are you *deliberately* omitting the father in your picture of the family?"[30]

The congregational polity of Episcopal churches allows such dissenting opinions to flourish. Although observing a uniform liturgy and order of worship, each congregation determines its own position on private-sphere issues. Its leaders, both lay and ordained, select their own forms of education and outreach, including teaching about family. Each congregation also develops its own internal culture and its own ethos or "congregational idiom" within the Prayer Book form of unity. In this regard, Episcopal congregations have far more autonomy than do Methodist congregations—a kind of individualism under the umbrella of corporate identity. In apparent contradiction, the *external* structure of liturgical order, providing a unanimity of gesture and text, also allows a highly individualist *internal* participation.

This seeming paradox helps explain why Episcopal congregations, in spite of historic associations of family with the larger society, have always attracted singles and loners, sometimes in larger proportion than nuclear families. Children, of course, represent "new life and continuity, a promise" to most congregations. "For all the comfort worshippers find in prayer," Nick Taylor writes in *Ordinary Miracles,* "for all the generosity and sharing preached in the Gospel, children [are indeed viewed as] the crux."[31] Paradoxically, however, Episcopalians have no unanimity of focus on family, faith formation, or pedagogy. Each congregation is left to evolve those issues in the best way it can—one might say, on its own.

Conclusion

Here we cite the language and imagery in the two prayers "For Families" found in the present *Book of Common Prayer* (1979). The first, written in 1883, expresses the consummate Victorian family ideal:

> Almighty God, our heavenly Father, who settest the solitary in families: we commend to thy continual care the homes in which thy people dwell. Put far from them, we beseech thee, every root of bitterness, the desire of vainglory, and pride of life. Fill them with faith, virtue, knowledge, temperance, patience, godliness. Knit together in constant affection those who, in holy wedlock have been made one flesh. Turn the hearts of the parents to the children, and the hearts of the children to the parents; and so enkindle fervent charity among us all that we may evermore be kindly affectioned one to another; through Jesus Christ our Lord, Amen.[32]

That angle of vision contrasts in multiple symbolic ways with the broad contemporary inclusivity of the prayer written especially for the 1979 edition:

O God, you made us in your own image and redeemed us through Jesus your Son: Look with compassion on the whole human family; take away the arrogance and hatred which infect our hearts; break down the walls that separate us; unite us in bonds of love, and work through our struggle and confusion to accomplish your purposes on earth; that in your good time, all nations and races may serve you in harmony around your heavenly throne, through Jesus Christ our Lord, Amen.[33]

A "household of grace" perspective for the twenty-first century understanding of family makes fitting "bookends" with the earlier prayer for the as-yet-unwritten Episcopal theology of family.

NOTES

1. Discos Tantalus, "Parental Government: A Privilege to Youth," *Churchman's Magazine* 4 (December 1807): 478–79. On the English patriarchal family worldview, see Lawrence Stone, *The Family, Sex & Marriage 1500–1800* (New York: Harper & Row, 1977).
2. Tantalus, "Parental Government."
3. Pastoral Letter quoted in Robert E. Hood, *Social Teachings in the Episcopal Church* (Wilton, Conn.: Morehouse Publishing, 1990), 138. Hood has compiled the first "core" of Episcopal teachings "informed by a theological understanding" (ibid., ix) from bishops' pastoral letters, General Convention reports, resolutions and memorials, and Lambeth Conference statements. This unique volume illustrates the "episodic, transient character" of Episcopal Church pronouncements and the "noticeable absence of sustained theological debate" (Hood's characterization, ibid., xviii).
4. Margaret Miles, "Theory, Theology, and Episcopal Churchwomen," in *Episcopal Women, Gender, Spirituality and Commitment in a Mainstream Denomination,* ed. Katherine Prelinger (New York: Oxford University Press, 1992), 335–36.
5. Frank Colquhoun, *Prayers for Every Occasion* (New York: Morehouse-Barlow, 1974), 200.
6. Reginald Heber, "From Greenland's Icy Mountains," in *Episcopal Church Hymnal* (1916), stanza 3, #476.
7. Hood, *Social Teachings,* xii.
8. Henry Caswall, *America and the American Church* (1839) (New York: Arno Reprints, 1969), 343.
9. Harriet Beecher Stowe quoted in Richard Bushman, *The Refinement of America* (New York: Alfred A. Knopf, 1992), 335, 340–41.
10. Bushman, *Refinement of America,* 323–30.
11. Cited in R. Bruce Mullin, *Episcopal Vision, American Reality* (New Haven, Conn.: Yale University Press, 1986), 215.

12. See Mary S. Donovan, *A Different Call: Women's Ministries in the Episcopal Church, 1850–1920* (Wilton, Conn.: Morehouse-Barlow, 1986).

13. An outgrowth of the Episcopal Family Network, itself authorized by a resolution at the General Convention in 1979, the *Episcopal Study on Clergy Families,* begun in 1986 and funded by the Church Pension Fund, Episcopal Church Foundation, and Trinity Church Grants, was published in 1988. It cited the contradictory self-understanding that the family "is the center" of the Episcopal identity when, in fact, individuals are the basic theological unit. Even clergy pray at home *as individuals* more often than with their families (author's italics).

14. Quoted in Clifford Putney, "Men and Religion: Aspects of the Church Brotherhood Movement, 1880–1920," *Anglican and Episcopal History* 63 (December 1994): 450–67, especially 458, n. 31. He saw Roman Catholicism as "entirely at variance with the dominant thought of our country and institutions."

15. Authorized by the 1946 General Convention and published by Seabury Press, New York, it included Robert C. Denton, ed., *The Holy Scriptures* (1951); Powell Mills Dawley, *Chapters in Church History* (1950); James Pike and Norman Pittenger, *The Faith of the Church* (1951); Massey Shepherd, *The Worship of the Church* (1952); Powell Mills Dawley, *The Episcopal Church and Its Work* (1955); and Stephen Bayne, *Christian Living* (1957).

16. J. B. Gillespie, "What We Taught: Christian Education in the American Episcopal Church 1920–80," *Anglican and Episcopal History* 56 (March 1987): 45–86.

17. Lambeth and Anglican Consultative Council, *Transforming Families and Communities: Christian Hope in a World of Change,* ed. Alan Nichols, Joan Clarke, and Trevor Hogan (Cincinnati, Ohio: Forward Movement Publications, 1988).

18. The Mormons were censured in the study, but the harsh words were removed in deference to African Anglicans at the worldwide gathering of Anglican Bishops in Lambeth England in 1988 (Hood, *Social Teachings,* 137ff).

19. Hood, *Social Teachings,* 148.

20. Prelinger, "Introduction," in *Episcopal Women,* 10.

21. Documents from the Youth Ministry Section, The Rev. Dr. Sheryl Kujawa, Department of Education, Evangelism & Ministry Development of the Executive Council, New York.

22. David Holmes, *A Brief History of the Episcopal Church* (Valley Forge, Pa.: Trinity Press International, 1993), 174–76.

23. Wade Clark Roof and William McKinney, *American Mainline Religion: Its Changing Shape and Future* (New Brunswick, N.J.: Rutgers University Press, 1987), see pp. 107–17 for a discussion on social class and pp. 209–17 for a discussion of "the new morality."

24. Terry Mattingly, "The Episcopal Church Makes for Good Press," *Living Church,* 14 September 1994, 11–13.

25. L. William Countryman, *Dirt, Greed and Sex: Sexual Ethics in the New Testament and Their Implications for Today* (Philadelphia: Fortress Press, 1988), 238–39, 256.
26. Tom Breidenthal, "Bodies Politic: Toward a Theology of Christian Households," *The Anglican: A Journal of Anglican Identity* 23:3–4 (Fall/Winter 1993/1994): 22–30.
27. Barbara Harris, Sermon at Province I Convocation, 17 November 1993, Rose Conference Center, Holyoke, Mass.
28. Lambeth and Anglican Consultative Council, *Transforming Families,* 61–66.
29. "ESA Urges Withholding Funds over Sexuality Issues," quoted from *Diocese of Rhode Island Episcopal News* 41 (November 1994): 14.
30. Rev. D. Locke Bowman, ed., *Episcopal Children's Curriculum,* 1991 (Alexandria, Va.: Virginia Theological Seminary and Morehouse Publishers). Incident related in telephone interview, March 1994.
31. Nick Taylor, *Ordinary Miracles: Life in a Small Church* (New York: Simon & Schuster, 1993), 323.
32. Marion Hatchett, *Commentary on the American Prayer Book* (New York: Seabury Press, 1980), page 565 discusses the prayer found on page 828 of the 1979 edition.
33. Ibid., 557, for a discussion of Charles P. Price's prayer written for the 1979 edition of *The Prayer Book* (p. 815).

11

Ecumenical and Interdenominational: Private and Public Approaches to Family Issues

EILEEN W. LINDNER

The ecumenical and interdenominational Christian witness on behalf of families during the last half-century was carried out by two pre-eminent agencies, the National Association of Evangelicals (NAE) and the National Council of the Churches of Christ, U.S.A. (NCCC). These agencies are not churches, so little attention is given here to doctrinal perspectives on the family. A rather broad range of theological traditions is represented among the membership of both organizations. Yet each agency came to represent a specific pole in the highly polarized debate over "family values" that has raged since World War II.

As the twentieth century draws to a close, the societal debate over family values has become the hallmark and most heated skirmish of the broader cultural wars in America. The nexus of issues and concerns corporately referred to as "family values" has served as the front line in the encounter between those perceived as conservative Christians and those perceived as liberals.

This bipolar analysis, however, proves too simplistic in describing the complex evolution of American Christian thinking regarding the family. A more adequate analysis may be found in assessing the degree to which groups of Christians began this half century raising children in conformity with the dominant themes of the culture but concluded it in firm opposition to them.

Further complicating the picture is the necessity of charting two distinct trajectories orbiting around the gravitational pull of the dominant culture, which was dramatically realigning itself throughout the period. The NAE and NCCC reflect the two dominant motifs of American Protestantism that have historically shaped the religious landscape of the nation. The first is rooted in the conservative, private tradition associated with fundamentalism; the other, in the progressive, public tradition of modernist theology. The content of their witness to the larger society on policy matters pertaining to the family has been shaped by these rich, but distinct, traditions to which each is heir.

Cooperative Christianity
at Mid-Century

The immediate post–World War II period in the United States gave rise among the churches to a renewed vigor, and it swelled the ranks of those who became active members of Protestant parishes throughout the country. This resurgence of religion can be measured by affiliation statistics, religious publications for the era, and in church construction. Although some of the boom in church construction can be attributed to the construction industry changing from wartime demand to peacetime, this alone does not fully explain the dramatic increase in building expenditures. In 1946, national figures record $76 million in church construction, escalating tenfold by 1956, and exceeding $1 billion by 1960.[1] Untold portions of this building explosion were devoted to the establishment of Christian education buildings adjacent to local churches amid the sprawling new housing developments that began to dot the suburban landscape. Families, especially young families, populated the churches in unprecedented numbers.

The postwar baby boom reconfirmed the affiliation patterns of American Protestantism. Young adults who had absented themselves from parish life since their teen years returned to parish life as parents to the largest age cohort in American history. The churches, presented with overwhelming numbers of families with young children and rejoicing in a revival of religious fervor and vitality, devoted much of their efforts to adapting programs, and even teachings, to the voracious appetite of this first postwar generation.

The specific response of the various denominations to the needs of families in the decades following World War II is recounted in other chapters of this book. They tell a tale of complex social organizations responding to rapidly expanding demands in a climate of economic optimism, political uncertainty, and cultural transformation.

This chapter considers the same era from the perspective of the two preeminent expressions of cooperative Christianity, which were themselves transformed by the same demographics and social changes that brought opportunity and challenge to denominational ministry to and with families. The NAE was founded in 1942; the NCCC in 1950. Neither agency was the product of the mid-century ethos; rather, each was rooted in issues and initiatives of an earlier era. The relationship of each of these organizations to the older fundamentalist-modernist controversy in American theology was to be determinative in guiding each organization's response to issues of the family in the decades to follow.

In the 1940s, *fundamentalism,* a term coined in its heyday two decades earlier, was experiencing the restive struggles of a movement that had seen its ranks swell throughout the Depression years. The number of adherents to the principles of fundamentalism not only increased but also diversified throughout the 1930s, although many, if not most, would avoid the designation "fundamentalist." Within that larger stronghold of conservative Christianity, the single commonality seemed to be a militant stance in opposition to modernism. Dispensationalists, Pentecostals, the holiness tradition, and more classical evangelical Protestants gathered in an uneasy, shared fellowship. Yet even in sober prewar America, the stern dispensational view chafed too tightly against those of classical evangelical sentiments, with their moderate Calvinist doctrine and enthusiastic cultural aspirations. This "positive evangelicalism" recalled its nineteenth-century appeal and sought to reclaim it for the sake of America's soul. One careful historian of these internal dynamics of fundamentalism in the 1940s describes those with reformers' instincts this way:

> the "new evangelical" reformers repudiated both the doctrinal and the cultural implications of a thoroughgoing dispensationalism while they remained loyal to the fundamentals of fundamentalism. . . . Their version of fundamentalism was defined primarily by the culturally centrist tradition of nineteenth-century American evangelicalism.[2]

This impulse to temper fundamentalism was nurtured by the hope of "winning" America for Christ.[3] Rather than steadfastly preserving doctrine, this movement promoted evangelism and sought to shed anti-intellectualism without giving in to modernism.[4]

Thus in the early 1940s, in the seedbed of fundamentalism there sprouted a group of gifted leaders who sought both to displace the liberalism that had come to dominate many of their denominations and, at the same time, to rid fundamentalism of its most brittle edges. Theirs was a search for a pandenominational institutional expression that would allow conservative Christians to work cooperatively and effectively within the nation's cultural and social context.

In 1941, the American Council of Churches (ACC) was founded as a fundamentalist counterpoint to the Federal Council of Churches. Characterized by strident anticommunism and anti-Catholicism, from its inception the ACC was polemical and narrow in its outreach, ultimately failing to capture the interests of neoevangelicals.[5] The conflicts of 1941 and 1942 that resulted in the founding of the ACC and the NAE respectively, represent the emergence of the evangelical movement as a force distinct from fundamentalism.[6]

By 1945, the NAE could claim only a million members from twenty-two church traditions, but it quickly signaled a new configuration of the religious landscape.[7] Mark Ellingsen, who carefully charted the growth of the modern evangelical movement, carries this analysis further in saying: "In some respects the National Association of Evangelicals is what created the Evangelical Movement as we know it today. . . . The NAE soon developed into a major symbol of the resurgence of the conservatives who found the 'Evangelical Spirit' congenial."[8]

If the framework of the NAE was rooted firmly in the fundamentalist-modernist controversy, so too did the Federal Council of Churches, taproot of the National Council of Churches, extend deeply into the loam of that controversy. At its founding in 1908, the Federal Council of Churches of Christ in America institutionalized the Social Gospel movement in much the way the NAE would later institutionalize the neo-evangelical movement.

An important and enduring distinction must be made between the American manifestations of conciliar ecumenism (the model of both the Federal and National Councils of Churches) and the NAE. As a coalition, the NAE has always offered membership to individuals, congregations, and denominations; not so conciliar ecumenism. With a highly developed sense of the ecclesial significance of ecumenical agencies, church councils have reserved membership for denominational churches. This has served the Christian unity theme of ecumenism and furthered the corporate emphasis of the liberal Protestant theology that undergirds many (but not all) those within the ecumenical movement.

Delegates from thirty-three denominations were present at the 1908 founding of the Federal Council of Churches, a triumph for those who proposed federation rather than organic union.[9] It also signaled the ascendency of liberal theology with its links to the practical and pastoral concerns of the social order. Historian Sydney Ahlstrom points out that whereas the Social Gospel fell far short of the radical liberalism it was sometimes thought to be, it did mark a sharp break from traditional evangelical Protestant thought and practice. The Social Gospel gained an important platform in American Protestantism and built an active monument to liberal, public, outward-oriented theology. Yet it largely failed to convert a significant number of its own coreligionists to the social dimensions of the gospel imperative.[10]

For the next forty years, criticism of denominational leaders and their liberal Social Gospel commitments was somewhat muted by the continued existence of numerous interdenominational agencies that provided an outlet for more traditional theological commitments. If the nascent conciliar ecumenism had abandoned the central evangelical calling of the gospel, at least, it could be argued, loyalty to those older commitments could be maintained through mission agencies and the like. While many members in the pews rejected or were suspicious of the Federal Council and its attention to urban and economic concerns, it had an influential following at seminaries and universities, as well as among mainline denominational leadership.

In the 1950s, conciliar ecumenism brought together specialized mission agencies through the formation of the National Council of the Churches of Christ in the U.S.A. The NCCC had immediately embraced several Eastern and Oriental Orthodox communions and historic African-American churches. The inclusion of these churches heightened Council attention to international concerns and the unresolved matter of race in American society. In 1950, the NCCC represented more than thirty-three million American Christians in nearly 150,000 parishes.[11]

By mid-century, two preeminent interdenominational and ecumenical agencies had emerged within Protestantism. The NCCC had a large membership and possessed a latent memory of the religious hegemony many of its member churches had long enjoyed. The NAE, with its sense of competitiveness, regarded the NCCC with great suspicion and preserved memories of a faith unaffected by modernism's unwelcome criticisms and questions.

These two agencies followed quite distinct trajectories to center stage in the Protestant drama in America, each seeking to be a prophetic voice in society, issuing resolutions crafted to bring the insights of Christianity to political, social, and spiritual problems. These resolutions more often than not would contradict each other, evidence that the central insights and issues of the fundamentalist-modernist controversy remained unresolved. Few issues illustrate this conflict in a more obvious way than the issue over the family and its place in modern society.

Formed following World War II to consolidate cooperative social action for their representative constituencies, both agencies lamented the changes in the postwar family. The NCCC typically attributed such changes to contemporary society. The NAE, in contrast, asserted that such problems arose primarily from individual failures of faith and diligence. In these early years both upheld monogamy, fidelity, gender-defined roles, and ordered authority. For both groups, the 1960s would provide a crucible for their own identity and for defining their relationship to culture.

The Struggle for
Public Voice and Moral Authority

The opening salvo in what would be an enduring contest for the public voice of American Protestantism regarding the family came even prior to the 1943 Constitutional Convention of the NAE. How and to whom would the airwaves of religious broadcasting (then radio) be allocated? What would be the content via the electronic bully pulpit of the religious message to be sent to families scattered across the nation?

The Federal Council of Churches, along with the Catholic and Jewish communities, had already established a tripartite sharing of the broadcast networks. Despite this, NAE proponents in negotiations with the broadcast industry managed to achieve their goal of gaining an electronic gateway to the families of America on behalf of conservative Protestantism.[12] When one reflects on this early encounter today and the subsequent evangelical use of broadcast ministry in both radio and television, it seems a vitally significant success. Liberal Protestants were to take note: A new voice for Protestantism was emerging.

Both agencies soon established offices in Washington to further advance their respective public, often opposing, voices.[13] The NCCC initially was more influential than the newer and smaller NAE.

However, during the 1960s, the NCCC increasingly devoted its attention to issues of race and civil rights, whereas the NAE devoted far more attention to overseas missions, evangelism, and Christian education endeavors. Such priorities made the NAE appear as either removed from the public controversy or favoring the status quo, in sharp contrast with the NCCC's progressive bent.

Although the NCCC and the NAE have consistently identified themselves as supportive of families and have developed a variety of approaches to family-related concerns over the past forty-five years, neither agency has yet developed a comprehensive policy concerning the family or sustained any ongoing program to address family concerns. Why, considering the lip service given to family concerns, is there an absence of such manifestations of commitment?

"Valuing" Family Values

Several factors may account for the paucity of initiatives regarding the family. One explanation may be the very nature of these ecumenical and interdenominational agencies. The lack of doctrinal unanimity among the members of each agency likely has inhibited their work in the family ministry field. Unlike a denomination, neither of these agencies held a set of ready-made precepts based on doctrine and tradition to pass on to their constituencies. Moreover, both agencies are one step removed from congregations and the theological seminaries, where so much of such programming is shaped. Implicit in the self-understanding of the NCCC and NAE is the notion that they serve as a locus for co-operative-action planning rather than a source of program operation.

In both the NCCC and the NAE, membership represents many diverse traditions, making any summary of teaching on such doctrinal matters as marriage, baptism, confirmation, or initiation difficult. In the case of baptism, for instance, both groups include constituents who practice infant baptism, as well as those who practice believers' baptism. The instruction concerning such family-related topics is therefore left to each specific denomination's tradition. This absence of consensus extended to such issues as divorce, mothers working outside the home, family discipline, sex education, and family economic stability make the formulation of program or policy elusive.

Another factor contributing to the lack of response to family concerns is inherent in the nature of the family itself. Especially early in the period under study, family concerns were considered a very private affair. Social research and analysis of the family were late in developing, and still carry a notoriously high margin of error owing to the taboo of violating the privacy within a family; they may also be perceived as calling into question the social organization and traditional distribution of authority within the family—patterns inherited in part from religious tradition.

A final factor in understanding the relative neglect of the family by ecumenical and interdenominational structures lies in the nature of the religious programming of the day. Despite considerable theological tension between conservative and liberal Christians of the era, some common practices can be observed across the theological divide. Especially in the 1950s and 1960s, church bureaucratic structures flourished in both theological camps. In some churches, one agency might deal with Christian education, a second with pastoral care, a third with women's mission agencies, and a fourth with youth work. A coherent and consistent approach to family was never quite achieved. Indeed, separate agencies within a single church might hold differing ideas of what family entails.

The protected status of family, encapsulated as it was within specific faith traditions, was seriously threatened with exposure during the turbulent 1960s. In that decade, a new perspective on such issues as premarital sex, divorce, adultery, cohabitation, drug experimentation, and male dominance appeared to erode the virtue of inherited traditional values.

Establishing a Two-Pronged Approach

Although family issues have never commanded the same degree of attentiveness as, for example, racial justice within the NCCC or evangelism within the NAE, the cultural pressures of the 1960s forced these agencies to address family issues. The NCCC and the NAE reflected a similarity of approach if not content.

Both the NCCC and the NAE have created coalitional structures through which to work to address the growing concerns over family. The NAE instituted a Family Commission, and the NCCC maintained a Family Life Committee (with changing designations for the latter group). Sharing responses and perspectives, these agencies offered members a forum in which to reflect on issues of the family in light of what seemed an unrelenting cultural siege. Under NCCC auspices, a series of conferences was held during the 1960s and 1970s.

In providing for such coalitional activity, both the NAE and the NCCC have provided highly valued services to their constituents by enabling their participants to enrich their own efforts at family ministry and to jointly publish curricular and other material. In each case, they have provided an important professional association for those working in family-related areas of ministry.

The NCCC and the NAE have also engaged in a number of public policy advocacy initiatives, motivated by a conviction of Christian moral witness in the society and exercising social responsibility in providing adequate support to families. The prominent place policy advocacy has occupied in the NCCC and NAE illustrates the importance both agencies give to addressing the changing cultural expectations and assumptions and the evolving definition of the family. However, although the methodology and approach is similar, the content differs.

From the mid-1960s to 1980, the number and forms of public policies that were designed to address or to deliver services to families increased exponentially. Such policies range from those that involve virtually every American family (such as the Internal Revenue Code) to those that address the special needs of the poor or the disadvantaged.

By and large, the NAE saw social policy on family issues as an unwelcome and destabilizing intrusion of government, as well as a threat to the family's role as instiller of religious values. For its part, the NCCC saw social policy as a means of providing necessary support to families in a changing world. Government, in this view, was benign, having a neutral impact on cultural and religious values of families.

Given the wide discrepancy of assumptions, it is not surprising that the NAE and NCCC were seen (and often saw each other) as opponents in a struggle for the soul of the American family. An issue would arise in which the NCCC would encourage governmental involvement and funding to families: aid to families with dependent children, various child-care and child health initiatives, and especially programs that provide birth control, sex education, or abortion funding. The NAE often opposed such government involvement as a disincentive to family determination to remain faithful to traditional forms and values. Only after the mid-1980s did these agencies adopt a more intentional approach to families, and the term "family values" began to assert itself.

Family Advocacy in
the Public Square

The Washington offices established early in the development of the NAE and the NCCC steadily grew in sophistication and strength. In addition to administering the day-to-day affairs of the interdenominational and ecumenical agencies, these offices developed sophisticated approaches to public policy advocacy and launched an effective public witness on a wide array of issues.[14] In addition to conveying the sentiment of the NAE or NCCC to legislators on timely social issues, these offices often alerted their respective agencies to self-interest concerns in pending legislation. They maintained ongoing relationships with congressional offices, as well as with each successive presidential administration, with varying degrees of success. The shifting political climate during these years had an obvious effect on the access and effectiveness of their Washington offices. To a degree, the NAE and NCCC offices vied for recognition as the legitimate voice of Protestant America, either a conservative or a progressive Christianity, particularly with regard to family issues.

Even where the NAE and the NCCC have agreed on a specific policy initiative, there have been discernable differences in their way of framing and arguing the question. The issue of abortion provides a case in point.

Throughout its history, the NAE has taken a strong and unequivocal stance in opposition to abortion and its inclusion in federally funded healthcare programs.[15] In the 1961 *Pronouncement* of its General Board titled "Responsible Parenthood," the NCCC also opposed abortion. In the text of this statement, special care was taken to identify internal differences among Orthodox and Protestant churches within NCCC membership. The statement characterized Protestantism as "condemning abortion . . . except when the health or life of the mother is at stake." But it left the door to abortion ajar: "The ethical complexities involved in the practice of abortion related to abnormal circumstance need additional study by Christian scholars."[16]

The NCCC revisited this perspective a decade later. Its own consensus had eroded, leaving it no longer able to reassert its opposition. Thereafter the NCCC maintained that economic status and dependency on governmental healthcare should not alter the medical services (including abortion) available to all women. From the outset, the NAE articulated its position clearly and directly, reflecting the greater theological and social consensus of that organization. The NCCC, with its broader theological diversity, was unable to establish let alone sustain an unequivocal position.

Sometimes the NAE and NCCC have agreed on public policy but are informed in their respective decisions by quite distinct understandings of Christian social ethics and distinct expectations of the body politic. The NAE has tended to have Christian teaching (particularly the evangelical perspective) weighed in the formulation of policy as a means of preserving the nation's religious heritage. The NCCC also seeks to preserve the nation's religious heritage (particularly the liberal Protestant perspective) by having government policy observe strict neutrality on ethical issues.[17]

The NAE and NCCC are also able to adopt diametrically opposed stances on the basis of ostensibly similar principles. The Equal Rights Amendment (ERA), at least marginally related to family matters, is a good example. Both had the same starting point: the first chapter of Genesis. Both were convinced that the dignity of male and female was derived from their Creator and attested to by biblical witness. Their difference, it appears, existed in the way in which the power of the state might best be utilized in relation to this value. In this instance, the NCCC favored strictly enforced equal treatment of men and women, whereas the NAE favored the continuation of traditional cultural practice, believing that no violation of human rights was jeopardized. In its concern to preserve the place and dignity of women, the NAE opposed the ERA, noting, "It could be interpreted to reach results antithetical to Judeo-Christian values."[18]

Thus both the NCCC and the NAE have long sought to bring the insights of Christian teachings to the business of formulating public policy and matters of governmental conduct. Neither agency shows evidence of being reluctant to speak from a faith basis in a secular context, but rather, both seem to regard doing so to be an act of Christian fidelity. Their relative position on any given issue is shaped by those theological perspectives and biblical understandings inherited from their past. In the two illustrations that follow, we can trace those deeper theological issues and concerns that lay behind their approach to family-related policy issues.

Public Education

Few matters are more central to a family than the education of its young. Churches too have a close tie with education in general and public education in the United States. Perhaps the corporate memory of the relationship between Sunday school and the development of public education explains in part an expectation on the part of churches that public schools are and should be repositories of the dominant (Christian) culture.[19] However, as time passed, public education was challenged by growing racial, religious, linguistic, and ethnic diversity, and from the mid-1950s onward by attempts to use the public schools as a primary vehicle to reverse racial discrimination and isolation. These factors placed public education on everyone's primary agenda—society, the churches, and the government. When this forty-year period began, both the NAE and the NCCC were in harmony, but as it came to an end, they found themselves diametrically opposed.

Throughout the 1950s and early 1960s, both the NAE and NCCC adopted resolutions opposing aid to parochial education, with NCCC adopting a policy in 1961 titled "Public Funds for Public Schools."[20] The NAE, still reeling from the much-opposed election of John F. Kennedy, a Catholic, to the presidency, asserted a similar view.[21] But this was where the agreement between the two agencies ended. They were strongly opposed in areas such as forced regionalization of school districts to assure racial desegregation (NCCC for, NAE opposed); prayer in the public schools (NAE for, NCCC opposed); and tuition tax credits for private education (NAE for, NCCC opposed).[22]

By the 1980s, the rift had become a chasm. In 1984, the NAE adopted a statement titled "Free Exercise of Religion in the Public Schools," which called for a constitutional amendment providing for voluntary school prayer and equal access legislation prohibiting discrimination against public high school groups on the bases of the religious content of their speech.[23] A year earlier, it had adopted a resolution encouraging tuition tax credits for those selecting private education, with the important caveat that such tax credit would apply only to schools demonstrably free of racial discrimination.[24] Nonetheless, the resolution came at a time in which "Christian academies," most of them evangelical in sympathy, were the fastest growing area of American education.

For its part, the NCCC in 1986 adopted a strong statement in support of the public schools and their funding. This statement stressed the importance of adequate revenues for education and the role of state and federal government in assuring the quality of public education.[25] In short, in the context of rapidly growing private sector education the NCCC pledged its support to public education.

It is evident from this that the NAE has been a strong and consistent supporter of government policies and programs within public education that support the nuclear family and reinforce cultural norms derived from the Judeo-Christian ethic. The NCCC, on the other hand, works to guarantee that schools will operate to ensure equity and the blessings of liberty to all citizens as a manifestation of public life and governance. These conflicting responses to public education mirror the "private" faith and "public" faith to which each of these agencies is heir. Although both groups are informed by their understandings of fidelity in the public arena, they bring divergent messages—both grounded in Christian theology—to the issue of public education.

Child Day Care

The issue of child day care provides another picture of contrasting approaches to family issues. From the mid-1970s onward, the NCCC became an advocate for child care or day care, as it more commonly was called. The NAE, to the contrary, resisted out-of-home placement, although it later modified its position.

A variety of factors contributed to a burgeoning of day-care centers in the 1970s: (1) delayed parenthood, which often meant mothers had established careers that they were reluctant to leave permanently; (2) economic pressure to develop dual-income families; (3) the birth of siblings several years apart, establishing a need for organized opportunities for socialization; (4) an increase in single-parent families in which the custodial parent had a need for employment; and (5) a decline in extended families under one roof, in which grandparents provide care to grandchildren.

In 1977, the Carnegie Corporation of New York produced a study titled, *All Our Children: The American Family under Pressure.* Its recognition of the wholesale transformation of families that is taking place, and its conclusion that all (not just "needy") families need support in raising children[26] played directly into the already sharp debates among secular liberal and conservative Americans. It strengthened the dividing line between Christian groups. The Carnegie study and others like it were perceived by the NAE as evidence of public encroachment on the private preserve of the family. The NCCC found new insight into how to work with families and children in a contemporary context.

The issue of out-of-home care for infants and preschool children became an acid test of family ideation. At stake was the concept of whether out-of-home care for the very young represented a dangerous social experiment or simply a timely adaptation of the family to meet contemporary needs. Throughout the 1970s, the NAE worked tirelessly to celebrate the virtue and importance of the stay-at-home mother and the wisdom of the inherited pattern of father-breadwinner, mother-nurturer. To many, including not a small number of those who out of perceived necessity utilized day care, this traditional family role expectation seemed self-evidently superior, as well as faithful to biblical norms. During the 1970s, the day care debate took place largely in church and mass media publications rather than in the legislative assembly halls (where the discussion revolved largely around Aid to Families with Dependent Children, commonly called "welfare").

In 1980, the NCCC undertook the largest study of child day care in America to this day. In doing so, it discovered that through direct sponsorship and use of space arrangements, churches constituted the largest single provider of child care in America.[27] The NCCC study indicated that although the church might wish to debate the merits of child care and its efficacy for the family, at the parish level the church was committing substantial resources to a childrearing pattern that already permeated American life. The study called on the church to focus its attention on quality child care and adequate compensation for day-care workers.[28] In 1984, the NCCC adopted a policy statement on Child Day Care that committed the churches to regulating the quality of the programs housed in churches and to actively advocating public policy support for child care.[29]

The NAE joined the alliance of pro-family groups opposing the federal funding of child care. It favored assuring tax credit provisions even for families that elected child care with religious content.[30] The NCCC, to the contrary, supported federal funding and federal standards in instances in which the NAE favored greater state discretion.[31] Here, as in the case of public education, its policy position was theologically rooted in a different understanding of what was in the best interests of families.

Conclusion

This survey of four decades of NAE and NCCC involvement in family issues reinforces historian Martin Marty's paradigm of "private" versus "public" understanding of the faith as applied to the issue of the family. Moreover, it indicates the way in which, over time, the flames were fanned in providing heat to the present cultural wars that divide the United States not only politically but religiously.

The issues, then, are ongoing. In 1990, the NCCC adopted a policy statement to guide those in pastoral ministry when dealing with families in which violence and abuse occur.[32] The NAE provided sponsorship for an extensive study of the needs of clergy families.[33] Both agencies continue to provide a forum for their constituents to meet and cooperatively plan in the area of family ministry, and to meet the ever-changing challenge to the family. Although the work of the NCCC and the NAE differs from that of denominations, as well as from one another, each has made substantial commitments to addressing family issues in contemporary society. Taken together, this legacy of family advocacy on the part of these two agencies has contributed an important chapter in the rich and diverse history of the Christian faith in relation to the American family.

NOTES

1. Sydney E. Ahlstrom, *A Religious History of the American People,* vol. 2 (Garden City, N.Y.: Doubleday & Co., 1975), 449.
2. George M. Marsden, *Reforming Fundamentalism: Fuller Seminary and the New Evangelicalism* (Grand Rapids: Wm. B. Eerdmans Publ. Co., 1987), 6. Marsden's history of the founding of Fuller Theological Seminary is the best to date of the emergence of neoevangelicalism from fundamentalism. Fuller, like the NAE, is one of the first products of that reforming process.
3. Perhaps the quintessential expression of this conquest is attributable to the first President of the NAE Harold J. Ockenga in his oft-cited speech, "Can Christians Win America?" *Christian Life and Times,* June 1947, 13–15.
4. Marsden, *Reforming Fundamentalism.* For a significant discussion of the intellectual redevelopment of evangelicalism, see Mark Ellingsen, *The Evangelical Movement: Growth, Impact, Controversy and Dialog* (Minneapolis: Augsburg Publishing House, 1988).
5. Marsden, *Reforming Fundamentalism,* and Ellingsen, *The Evangelical Movement.* Both point to the stark differences in posture among conservative Christians that led to the formation of the NAE despite the existence of the ACC. Further detailed exploration of the ACC approach is to be found in Erling Jorstad, *The Politics of Doomsday: Fundamentalists of the Far Right* (Nashville: Abingdon Press, 1970).
6. Arthur H. Matthews, *Standing Up, Standing Together: The Emergence of the National Association of Evangelicals* (Carol Stream, Ill.: NAE, 1992), 13. This is a nuanced account of the emergence of evangelical thought and practice.
7. Marsden, *Reforming Fundamentalism,* 50.
8. Ellingsen, *The Evangelical Movement,* 102.
9. Robert T. Handy, *A History of the Churches in the United States and Canada* (New York: Oxford Press, 1977), 305–7.
10. Ahlstrom, *A Religious History,* vol. 2, 272–73.
11. Handy, *A History of the Churches,* 406.
12. For a lively account of the NAE's struggle with the Federal Communications Commission and the radio networks, see Elizabeth Evans, *The Wright Vision* (Lanham, Md.: University Press of America, 1991).
13. A fine account of the work of both Washington offices can be found in Allen D. Hertzke, *Representing God in Washington: The Role of Religious Lobbies in the American Polity* (Knoxville: University of Tennessee Press, 1988).
14. Ibid.
15. James DeForset Murch, *Co-Operation Without Compromise: A History of the*

National Association of Evangelicals (Grand Rapids: Wm. B. Eerdmans Publ. Co., 1956).

16. General Board of NCCC(USA), *Responsible Parenthood,* adopted 23 February 1961, 2.

17. This is illustrated in the controversy over the appointment of a Vatican envoy/ambassador. See "A Brief on Diplomatic Representation at the Vatican," adopted by the NCCC(USA) General Board, 17 January 1951 and "Position of the National Council on Nomination of an Ambassador to the Vatican," adopted 31 October 1951. With regard to the NAE's extensive involvement in this issue, see Matthews, *Standing Up, Standing Together,* 90–91.

18. National Association of Evangelicals pamphlet, *NAE Resolutions: Selected Resolutions Adopted by the NAE During the Past Four Decades,* 1987, 18.

19. Robert Lynn and Elliott Wright, *The Big Little School* (Nashville: Abingdon Press, 1980).

20. General Board of the NCCC(USA), 13.4, *Minutes,* 8–9 June 1961; see also 13.1, *Church State Issues in Religion and Public Education,* 20 May 1953, and 13.2, *Federal Aid to Education,* 18 May 1954.

21. Matthews, *Standing Up, Standing Together,* 137–38.

22. The collected policy statements of both the NCCC and the NAE are easily accessible. The *Minutes* of the General Board of the NCCC(USA) and the *Selected Resolutions Adopted by the NAE,* cited above, contain complete references.

23. *Summary of NAE Resolutions,* 19.

24. *Summary of NAE Resolutions,* 27.

25. "Elementary and Secondary Public Education in the Society," in NCCC(USA), *Minutes,* 22 May 1986, 2.

26. Kenneth Keniston, *All Our Children: The American Family under Pressure* (New York: Harcourt, Brace, Jovanovich, 1977), 22.

27. Eileen W. Lindner et al., *When Churches Mind the Children* (Ypsilanti, Mich.: High/Scope Press, 1983) reports the extensive data of this study of over 100,000 parishes.

28. Ibid., 103–4.

29. General Board of the NCCC(USA), 7 November 1984, 39.1–10.

30. Curran Tiffany in private correspondence with the author, 11 July 1994.

31. The actual title of the "ABC Bill" was "The Child Care and Development Block Grant Act of 1990."

32. General Board of the NCCC(USA), *Minutes,* 31.2–1-2–4, 14 November 1990.

33. This effort has been spearheaded by and reported on by Lynne Dugan, a staff member of NAE's Office of Public Affairs, in Washington.